The Other Woman

by
Shirley R. Simeon

Bloomington, IN Milton Keynes, UK

Parity

AuthorHouse™
1663 Liberty Drive, Suite 200
Bloomington, IN 47403
www.authorhouse.com
Phone: 1-800-839-8640

AuthorHouse™ UK Ltd.
500 Avebury Boulevard
Central Milton Keynes, MK9 2BE
www.authorhouse.co.uk
Phone: 08001974150

All places, locations, institutions are factual including dates or circa dates. However, certain names have been changed.

© 2006 Shirley R. Simeon. All rights reserved.

No part of this book may be reproduced, stored in a retrieval system, or transmitted by any means without the written permission of the author.

First published by AuthorHouse 8/8/2006

ISBN: 1-4259-4015-3 (sc)
ISBN: 1-4259-4017-X (dj)

Printed in the United States of America
Bloomington, Indiana

This book is printed on acid-free paper.

Thanks to all of those who tirelessly listened to me talk about this project, read excerpts, edited in both professional and non-professional ways, cautioned me about the risk factors, but never, ever dissuaded me from completing it. From my psychotherapist to my Polish housekeeper of 16 years (whom I taught to speak English), from friends of my very first college, to colleagues of my own Psychology peers, from theater folk, where I maintained subscriptions, to Playwrights, from sales associates in the high-end stores where I would occasionally splurge, from friends of 60 years to a special friend of two years and all of the in-betweens. I thank you one and all. Special thanks goes to Dr. Clenora Hudson-Weems, professor of English at UMC, who served as a constant mentor and editor from day one.

Table of Contents

Prologue	1
Part I: Family	11
1920 - Grandparents	14
1929 - Uncles and Aunts	18
1930 - Life with Mother and Daddy	23
1934	30
1946-1960: Marriage - The Beginning & the End	33
Soliloquy	47
Part II: The Women	49
1938: The English Teacher	52
1942: Lil Harper	65
1955: Blanche	69
1956: Elaine	78
1968: Blanche, Part II	91
The Ride to O'Hare: Elaine and Blanche	97
1965: Sylvia, My Soul Mate	102
1968-1979: Blanche	110
1969: Bernice Wolfson	112
1969-1978: The Good Life	114
1974-1976: The "Other Blanche"	117
A Distraction: The Other Blanche	121
Blanche: The Transition	124
1999: Elaine, the Doctor/President	130
Part III: Revelations	135
Appendix: New Revelations	143

Prologue

December 6, 2000---9:30 PM
Whew! Well, that's that. Now is the time for some relaxation. Funeral is done. Peter is airborne or maybe even home by now. I flip on CNN. I am half-listening and half-looking. It's my time to just settle in and enjoy my own privacy. All of a sudden I experience excruciating pain- "…ouch, ouch." I grab my head and put my fingers on my temples. A fierce pain runs through both sides: unyielding, penetrating. I get up and move about the room. I search out a heating pad, then think, no-maybe an icepack will be better. I fling myself across the bed but the pain will not let me lie still. Then off I go to the medicine cabinet. No, I tell myself, better not take any painkillers until you know what you're doing.

I can call Weinstein, ask him.

December 7---12:30 AM
"Dr. Weinstein, I have a strange pain that won't go away. I've tried everything. It's so bad, I can't stay still. Which one of my three left-over-from-hip surgery-painkillers should I take? Ouch! There it goes again. If I didn't know better I'd think someone shot me through the temples."

"Take Nothing. Got to ER as quickly as possible and don't drive."

December 7---2:00 AM
My temperature registers at 103.5, I am experiencing lower chest and back pains. Admission is automatic.

December 7-11

Treated for aspiration pneumonitis. Chest X-rays are taken, a fluid tap, I am given antibiotics, then discharged with a prescription.

December 12-18

At home, condition worsens. I call Weinstein and he advises me to return to the hospital the next day.

December 19-27

Every diagnostic procedure available is utilized: daily medical visits, daily X-rays, daily blood smears, a cardiovascular stress test, a Doppler ECHO, electrocardiograms, CT scans of the abdomen, and of course blood pressure and temperature readings every few hours and dozens of consultations. They are keeping an eye on me!

I stay a week. I am treated for pneumonia. Given antibiotics and sent home. At home condition worsening. My temperature is registering at 103.5. Readmission to hospital is imminent. Every diagnostic procedure available is again utilized—alas, the angiogram, which furnishes the answers and ends the mystery. No, it isn't pneumonia; it is an aneurysm. A localized, pathological blood-filled dilation of a blood vessel, and what a blood vessel—the aorta!

My family has gathered to hear from the medics—my sons Roy and Peter, my sister Joy, and my cousins Beth and Amy. They are all here, some having come from long distances, in record time and at exorbitant costs. The medics have gathered with their timetables miraculously coordinated. What a feat! They too are all there—my cardiologist, my internist, and the surgeon. The hospital room suddenly turns into a classroom, a Q & A event with the surgeon at the blackboard graphically illustrating the status of my heart. The cardiologist speaks finally, training his eyes on me.

"You have an aneurysm of the aorta which is dissecting from and ascending down to the thoracic region. Your hemoglobin has fallen from 40 down to 25. In other words, the news is not good. Mortality rate is 50-60 % against you but without surgery, survival is 100% against you. The operation will take 8 to 9 hours without by-passes, longer with."

"So I have little or no choice, eh?"

My thoughts turn to dying and I begin to prepare for that. Family members are silenced and leave quietly, one by one.

* * *

How does one prepare to die? Let me count the ways: first, you deny the possibility, and I did. Then you pray, pray, pray, and I did. I surprised myself by remembering the words of my childhood prayers, my Catechism and Sunday school lessons.

Next, you dare to think of your own life, and I did. Was it bland, uneventful, or much too eventful? Did I finish anything? Did I produce anything? Should I have gone in another direction? Who will remember me? Who will quote me? Maybe none of that matters.

Seventy-seven is a high number and speaks to a long life. Maybe it's enough to have had those years pile up. Maybe that alone is a feat. Why do people worry so much about a Legacy? Why should I keep going back? Trying to make something I thought was important sound important to others?

The connection: that's what it is! Imagining that the reader might smile when he or she spots something they did but never put in print and glad to discover that someone has done it for them. So, I am going to prepare for dying by going back, way back, and maybe I won't even think about the awful surgery ahead of me.

My state of musing interrupted. The reverie delayed.

* * *

"Shirley, we are going to do the operation now; we can't wait until tomorrow. Sorry about your sons. I'll give a call to them. By the way, where is your rosary? I guess you left it in the room. I'll go get it."

Who says doctors don't listen to their patients? What a prize of a doctor I have!

They were always going to be there but it didn't happen the way they had planned. The results of the angiogram have moved the scheduled time for surgery to emergency. So no one is here to say "goodbye, good luck, and chin up" as they roll me into the butcher shop with no one but the surgical team. Family is telephoned to tell of the change and everyone stops in their tracks to take whatever means of transportation is available. The cutting and hacking has already begun before they arrive and all they can do is sit and bite their nails. Thirteen hours of nail biting!

Roy, son number one, wants to do his nail biting in his own home where he will have the emotional support of his wife and son, and he desperately wants his brother with him.

Peter is in conflict; he feels he belongs in the hospital with me but is immensely flattered that Roy needs him. Later he will tell me, "Mom, I've waited all my life for Roy to need me." So he proposes a compromise. "I'll go home with you rather than sitting in the hospital if we can make a short detour. I want to stop by Mom's apartment." Roy agrees and sits in the car while Peter races the elevator to the 14th floor.

Peter will tell me later that he came to my space to pray, not to God, but a pleading prayer to me. "Mama: don't leave me now. Please don't leave me now. Hang in there. You can do it. Live! Don't let them take you away—"

* * *

Peter has clung to me forever. It is as though he knew intuitively that he was not a "wanted" child when he began his life in my womb, that he was interrupting something—something major. I was in grad school and reveling in the glory of finally having been admitted to my beloved and coveted University of Chicago. In addition, the State of Illinois had awarded me with a sizeable stipend. Both were at risk with the pregnancy and both were cancelled, lost. Even if Peter was not clairvoyant, he had heard the story dozens of times and it appeared that he was determined to keep himself in my world no matter what it took. And for me to be removed from his world was unconscionable.

As his birth was "intrusive" the pattern of intruding continued in his life with me. Whenever anything special was happening to me, he would present an emergency of his own. For example, he had a life threatening asthma attack while working as a camp counselor in the north woods of California, which brought me to his bedside and cancelled a planned vacation. And there were many other similar episodes. Of course, he wanted me to live on after that infamous night of the surgery. I was his lifeline and later I came to regard him as a real treasure.

Not so with Roy; he was born at a different time and of a different marriage. Roy came into the world very much wanted—a Baby Boomer as we call his generation today. The world was beginning to be at peace and having children was proof that the country had returned to "normalcy." From early on my relationship with Roy was tenuous, suspect, with denial and lots of shadowboxing. How can a young mother shadowbox with her firstborn? What could I have been denying?

Roy was difficult, a perpetual challenge. At age three in a fit of anger, he threw a toy on the glass top of a coffee table while we were visiting his Great Aunt. As a young child he did poorly in Catholic school and when I pursued a private school for him and he was admitted, he chose "the least of them" for his friends—other borderline children. In high school he was on the edge of gang life, but not officially a member; he neither carried nor owned a weapon, did not use drugs, just presented himself as a surly adolescent with a chip on his shoulder. Yet his greatest anti-social behavior was truancy.

When I could no longer bear it, I "forced" him to join the military. I still cannot believe he permitted me to do that to him. He could have resisted just like he resisted all my other demands, but he didn't. I can only guess that he, like me, wanted to get out of harm's way. He had endured his father's indictment for a senseless crime, subsequent unemployment and then divorce, and now he was living in a strange situation with his mother and her women friends who seemed to be taking huge amounts of her time and attention.

His curiosity must have been killing him, for I discovered under his bed sheets one night a book entitled "Women Lovers." That clued me in to his anger. That clued me in to his truancy.

As it turned out he learned about "women lovers" in his own time. He learned by experiencing life with his mother and two women she loved—one who became a national figure and the other who lifted his mother into a whole new world of high-end culture and cuisine and endless professional opportunities, all of which he would come to share.

* * *

My eyes are as heavy as lead. I need my fingers to open them so that I can reassure my waiting relatives that I have indeed survived the surgery: that I am still alive. Prayers have been answered. The Intensive Care Unit has become my new home instead of the crematorium. I cannot move, can barely breathe. I never see my swollen feet and legs and so I don't know what people mean when they exclaim joyfully about the fluid having diminished. The T.I.A. (transient-isocheim attack) occurred only minutes before the surgery began and lasted only seconds. A mini-stroke, alas! --The significance of which will reveal itself later.

I'm still alive so I must endure bad food and dozens of medical students and interns bending over me and asking the same questions over and over again. I must practice restraint—plenty of restraint because there is nothing I can do about anything. I am a captive. I am incarcerated, but amazingly, I am alive. I wonder what would be going on today if I had not survived the operation. Would they be discussing the services? Would they be upset about my request for cremation? To some, cremation feels like paganism, especially to Catholics, and my family is a Catholic family. Would they find everything they would be looking for? Would there be arguments over my possessions that may not have been clearly designated in my Will? I don't think they would argue. They are a pretty civilized bunch of people and they have their own stuff. They wouldn't need to fight over mine.

I'm still alive, I keep telling myself as though even I don't believe it, living at the will of others. Now it's physical therapy which is strictly enforced and begins early each day. Mary--a loud, slaphappy buffoon, who typifies black stereotypes and makes white people laugh--leads the routines. The food pretends to be that which was ordered from the menu the day before but is often unrecognizable. I select orange juice on the double for breakfast but must explain why I don't want a full service meal; all day I'm explaining. Nurses and doctors tell me to eat. They weigh me. They frown. The next meal comes. The last meal is still on the tray.

After 3 PM I can rest, read and nap. All institutional requirements have been met. Now, about the phone—I really don't want to talk to anyone but they want to talk to me. They need reassuring, but I tire of their questions. Again, I am impotent. Not only can I do nothing about the therapy and the food, I cannot stop the phone. On second thought, I should be glad to have people calling me. They mean well. I could ask the receptionist to take messages but I won't.

I'll just enjoy the luxury of being able to lie here and remember days gone by—thinking about my mother and my brother who have passed on. Glad my mother was spared having to live through this surgery. I remember when I underwent emergency surgery at age 17 for a ruptured appendix replete with peritonitis and Mother traveled on public transportation across town each and every day after work to visit me. I wonder why all my surgeries have to be emergency events.

My brother was younger than I but always felt like an older brother to me. He worked from age 9, knew the value of a dollar and was never without one. Consistently he bailed me out of first one financial crisis and then another as I floated through life on dreams and promises and other such fluff. Steve had real street smarts, though he would not have liked the "Women" section of my book. He tried to understand the "woman thing" in my life but he never could get it. It wasn't that it alienated me from him; we were good friends until the end.

* * *

Now, I am much too sick to fuss about the tongues of the caregivers. If they will come when called and do for me what I cannot do for myself, then that is enough. My greatest pleasure is in daily visits from my relatives who reflect in their faces the condition of my recovery, and who keep me informed about my life "out there," bringing messages, mail, receipts from paid bills—none of which I read but all of which I welcome. And so I welcome my reflections of the events of my past, what has led me to the point I am at in my life now, and which I share with the world.

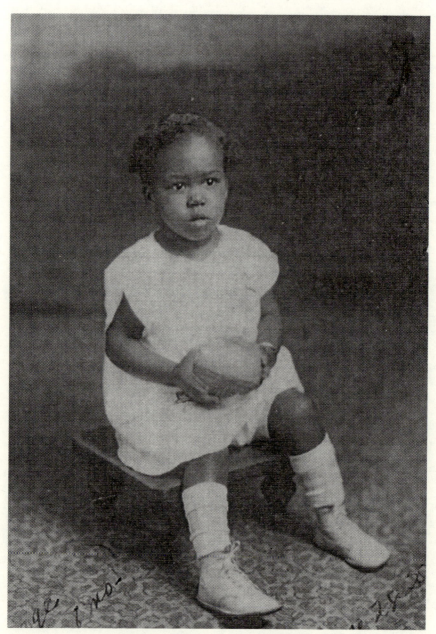

Shirley RIta at age 20 months

Part I:

Family

Oh, what a family I had! Their values and policies stretched from the ends of liberal thinkers and compassionate people to the other extreme—racists, sexists, and elitists. They contributed significantly to my development—from both extremes. On the one hand they were hardworking, tax paying citizens, great parents and surrogate parents and extended family role players. On the other hand, they were super-critical, high-minded, ambitious, striving and struggling to "get ahead of the next guy."

They took a good deal of pride in their work. It placed them in enviable situations where they would otherwise never have been. An uncle worked as the maitre'd in the famous Empire Room of what we would term today as a 5-Star Hotel, The Palmer House, and hob-knobbed with celebrities and performing artists from all over the world: Sonja Henie, the world-class skater of that day; Veloz and Yolanda, internationally famous dancers; Chester Gould, who wrote the comic strip "Dick Tracy" that was, and still is, syndicated all over the globe. In fact, not only did this uncle see these celebrities on a regular basis but he also made it possible for me and my brother to see them perform. And when my brother was a mere high school student he worked part-time in the Empire Room and collected autographs as well as tips. A high time for him was when he obtained Gould's autograph.

Undaunted by prejudice and racial discrimination, my parents and other family members took me everywhere: my father to Lincoln Park (from the south side where we lived) where I learned to row a boat, my aunt to the University of Chicago's Midway Plaisance where

I learned to ice-skate, an uncle to the racetracks where I learned to read the Mutual Boards. It was endless what I was exposed to.

Today my family would be called ugly names. Why? It would be said that they were emulating the white man because they spoke good English. They would be accused of denying their blackness because they do not wear rags on their heads, nor do they put their hair in pickininny-like braids, and the myriad of other trappings of so-called Black Culture, which is no culture at all.

My mother was truly exemplary of modern womanhood. While she held to her beliefs as a devout Catholic, old-world conservative, when I married in 1946 in the wake of World War II it was she who took me to one of the first Planned Parenthood clinics in Chicago because she knew I was not ready to have children.

I wonder how she would respond to my life, and particularly my account of it. If her responses to other things were any indication, I think she would have been just fine with it after an initial outcry. She had a curious way of disapproving, and then accepting, whenever any of us children did anything a bit off-color. Not just accepting in a give-in way—defeatist, but almost enjoying the off-color parts and finding a way to talk about them without making them into a scandal. We did many off-color things, both while we were knuckled under her control and afterwards. My brother brought a Spanish girl friend home from a golf trip once; that raised her eyebrows, but no shock and no reprimand. I was once involved with a very old and very rich man who purchased a luxury car for me. With great excitement I took the car to her house to show it off. The purchaser was hardly mentioned as we all found the fact of the car awesome; again, no reprimand. And when my affair with Blanche was cemented and the plan to relocate to California was definite, the more than 100 letters I received at the home of my mother barely got a comment.

Yes, I believe the entire family would find this book intriguing and enjoy every word of it without agreeing to the premise. They have that talent.

1920 - Grandparents

Going way, way back we land in Provident Hospital on the south side of Chicago where a tiny bundle of joy, a brown girl with a bald head, had just been delivered into the world. She was the firstborn into a family of doting relatives at a time when the country was relatively calm, and her family could afford her.

I was that girl and the time was 1923 under the drab administration of President Calvin Cooleridge, "Racism" (the phrase had yet to be coined) was an accepted way of life, black people were not offended when called "colored," but were when called "black." This was a time when segregation was legal, and few black folk lived in the north but were beginning to migrate.

It was the day of Booker T. Washington and W.E.B. Du Bois, and, of course, Cab Calloway and Lena Horne. The "invisible blacks" as defined by Ralph Ellison (in his award-winning self-titled book) were creating opportunities out of legal segregation. Quietly and without much notice, they were building a steady, solid middle class, which whites would not come to notice for many years hence. They were getting educated, becoming journalists, inventors, teachers, tradesmen (never mind that they were not permitted to join the unions), doctors, lawyers, statesmen and entrepreneurs.

The little brown girl who had just been delivered into the world had an entrepreneur Daddy and Grandpa. My grandparents made a factory out of their basement where they manufactured, packaged, sold and distributed porters' supplies among the valet shops and hotels of downtown Chicago. The basement was the lower level of their sixteen-room house that by the standards of that day could easily have been called a mansion.

At 553 East Browning Avenue, in front of an imposing gray stone on the south side of Chicago, sat an Auburn automobile, which my grandmother forbade my grandfather to take out when it rained. The supplies: shoe polish and dyes, rags and whiskbrooms were put on a delivery truck with a sign painted on the door—"C.H. Green & Son." My father was the "Son" who drove the truck and delivered the supplies, and on Saturdays when school was out, I went with him.

Grandma Green was considered to have been a striking woman— smooth, light brown complexion, silky gray hair styled with a side part and cut to a length just below her ears. When I visited her she was always dressed, replete with jewelry and sometimes wearing an apron when she had just taken a cake out of the oven. I never saw her slopping around her house in slippers and barelegged. Grandma gave off a cold, haughty persona and I don't remember ever seeing her laugh out loud.

She was a pillar at Grace Presbyterian Church whose membership boasted of Judge Wendell Green (no relation to us), Chicago's first black judge, and Maudelle Bousfield, Chicago's first black public school principal, and many other black "firsts." Grandma herself was a "first" of a sort since she graduated from Fisk University in the first class of graduates circa 1870.

Grandpa Green derived from a Virginia slave family and had no formal education but he had an unwavering determination to rise above his beginnings, and after migrating to Chicago began immediately to work for himself only. How he and Grandma met and married remains a mystery in the family. Four children were born of the marriage, my father being "Number Two" who dropped out of high school to work for Grandpa and drive the truck. Daddy was a tall, dark-skinned Negro man who became known as a fashion plate. His truck driving clothes were shed after a day's work. He always changed for dinner.

The "Number One" offspring of the Grandparents was Helen, a dutiful, compliant, angel-of-a-daughter who had a good marriage and four children. "Number Three" was the maverick daughter, Lucy. She had a mannish, tough demeanor, with a raucous laugh and wore a green shade cap which I lusted after. In today's world, she would have been your stereotypical lesbian. In 1930, she was just Lucy who could fix anything and change an automobile tire on the open road. The baby of the clan, Dick, had a short and tragic life. Though unbelievably privileged—expensive clothing of the British tradition, handsomely crafted toys—he did poorly in school and sought the streets where drugs found him and ultimately took him over. He overdosed at 17.

My maternal grandparents were quite different. My grandpa had died years before I was born and family gossip told that he was an Irish bastard child but he had married my grandma and all eleven of their children were legitimate.

Grandma was a peasant domestic servant from a French village called Potosi, sixty miles north of St. Louis. She lived a rural life in a country town until the last of her children left for Chicago and ultimately sent for her.

Mother's older sister and brother-in-law lived right down the street from my father's "mansion," but the circumstances were very different. Having come to Chicago first, they sent for my mother and a younger sister. They became parents to them, seeing them through high school. When Grandma Green learned that her son Steve had proposed marriage she came to call on mother's "parents." It was the older sister and brother-in-law who answered the call presenting my mother as the prize she was—a beauty of 21 years, a high school graduate, a dental hygienist, and unscathed. They married April 26, 1922. I was born October 13, 1923.

1929 - Uncles and Aunts

It's hard to imagine that a black child born in America in 1923 could be "privileged." It's even more amazing to think of dance school, recitals, chiffon pleated dresses and kid gloves for her, especially since she was not wealthy. But unimaginable as it was, that was my lot. I had it all.

"Hold still. I don't want to burn you."

In a black kitchen, so well illustrated by the artist Annie Hall, I sat as an almost-six-year-old on a telephone book in a high chair that hoisted me to the right height for hairdressing. My mother, who was using a hot iron comb, had just spoken. I had jumped, startled when I heard heels clacking down the long hall of the apartment. My fidgeting was making my mother's work with my hair a burn risk. The clacking heels on the wooden floor were bringing my beloved aunt to the kitchen.

"Hello, I brought you something—something special," and Terher in her excitement began to tear open the gift wrapping, revealing a pair of brown kid gloves fit for a princess. My mother gave her sister a discerning look of disapproval.

"Martha (Terher was my nickname for her), why would you buy kid gloves for a five year old? She doesn't need them. They won't even keep her hands warm."

"Della, you paid $16 for a chiffon dress she'll wear in the recital next month and perhaps never again. So what's the difference?

The recital at the Coliseum

Isn't she our family treasure? You've got your hands full with that baby boy." I had since acquired a brother.

"When do you feel is a good time to go skating, Terher?" I asked. I could raise my head now; the hairdressing was finished.

"Not until after the recital. I don't want to take the chance of your falling down and breaking your neck before."

"But, Terher," I protested, "I want to go skating today. Please don't make me wait until after the recital."

It really was a big deal, this recital. The dance teacher, Hazel Thompson Davis, had studied under the legendary Josephine Baker and was staging the recital in the palace of grandeur—the Coliseum. To perform in one of her recitals one had to be special, and I guess I was—at least to Terher. The skating was postponed.

* * *

When I entered school, the stock market stood at its all-time peak. On September 2, 1929, a single share of Montgomery Ward sold for $466; the previous year it was worth $132. In a month, panic would strike and America would be in the most serious economic decline of the century.

Everyone talked about being "laid off" and standing in "the bread lines out there."

Despite the talk, there were regular meals at our house, eaten in family style on tablecloths with napkins, though the meal itself was often a single dish. There were music lessons and money was found for Girl Reserve fees and Boy Scout uniforms. Birthdays and holidays were always celebrated ritualistically. Christmas was a fantasy of gifts and seldom was a practical, needed item included—no coats or shoes or sweaters under the tree.

My childhood world was a black world but it did not seem dark and dismal. In a curious way, it was balanced. While all the kids at school were black, all the teachers were white. While all our neighbors were black, white janitors lived in the apartment buildings with black tenants. Streetcar conductors, motormen, and policemen—all white. The laundry man, white, stoop-shouldered and flat-footed. The iceman, the hucksters driving wagons up and down the alleys, white.

Black men were denied those jobs, so an army of dumb, white men worked and lived among blacks. All our men folk had jobs and some of the women, too. They worked as servants, butlers, valets, chauffeurs, maitre d's, waiters, dining car porters on trains. Black women worked as maids and cooks. While wages were shockingly low, there were other perks for black people and their families—many others. We kids were kept informed of the major cultural events in the city because Uncle Will was the headwaiter at the Empire Room.

Performing artists from all over the world delighted and entertained us, performers our friends had never heard of. Tihi (our name for our Aunt Flora) worked for a coal magnate family as a full-time maid and she purchased my graduation dress as a gift with the charge plate of her employer. Another uncle was a Pullman porter on the Rock Island Railroad. When his marriage ended he came to live with us and it was like having Santa Claus in the house.

Uncle George worked in the dining car and made big tips, and when he came off his run to and from Toronto he would spread his tips across the dresser in his room, gesturing to us that tomorrow we would have a great lunch at school. He had heard us whining about a bicycle. Would you believe he purchased two bicycles: one for my brother and one for me? The day the Fair Store delivered them to our house would be a bigger thrill than the day I drove my first new car out of the Chevrolet showroom years later.

Uncle George was indeed a "sport." It was he who escorted my mother to see the prizefights in Chicago. He took me to the races and taught me how to read the Mutual Boards, taught me how to play poker, and secretly dashed me off to the barbershop to get my hair cut. "You can't ride well with all that long hair blowing in your face," he would say.

1930 - Life with Mother and Daddy

My mother, Della, was a superb mother who sacrificed everything for her children and molded them into what she thought would be successful people. No Nobel Prize winners among the three of us. No Poet Laureates, but she had her own criteria. She would say, "I got three out of three," when describing her luck of the draw. "They all finished school. Nobody got pregnant. Nobody ever spent a night in jail." For mother, that was successful parenting. It may still be.

I was seven years old and in the second grade in 1930 and only three days after my seventh birthday party the whole world seemed to be in crisis because the stock markets had crashed. The news was on everyone's lips and playing over our Philco. radio but it didn't have much meaning to my family. We did not lose fortunes because we did not have fortunes.

Black people had not invested in the stock markets. In fact, few even knew what the stock markets were. Their reference to the stock markets was the stockyards, the slaughterhouses on 35th street, back-of-the-yards where many blacks worked. Certainly, there were no black people committing suicide because all of a sudden, like overnight, they had become poor. No way. Most black folks were already, as expected, poor.

I lived in a large, spacious apartment on the south side, #5304 Prairie Avenue. My mother and father shared the apartment with my mother's two sisters and brothers-in-law. There were three bedrooms off a long hallway, a large kitchen and dining room, a butler's pantry and a regular pantry. There was a closed-in back

The "stair steps"

porch with stairs leading to a big backyard where kids could play on the grass. No ghetto!

Parents would call their children in from play by screaming their names from the banisters of the porches. There were five other apartments in this building, and in the parlance of the times, it was referred to as a "six-flat building." Our flat was on the second floor. A neighbor who was to become a celebrity—Mami Hansberry called her children in from play just like my mother and aunts called us in. The Hansberry family became celebrities when the father won a fight in the Chicago City Council against Restrictive Covenant, and much later when the youngest child, Lorraine, wrote and produced the legendary and award-winning play "A Raisin in the Sun."

* * *

With three women in the house, all bustling around the kitchen, I had few chores to do. Keep out of the way, dry the dishes, and put my things away—clothing, books, and toys—were my duties. Having pets in the house was viewed as a no-no. Occasionally we would bring in a stray dog or cat, hide it under the beds and feed it secretly until Mother discovered it and cast it out. The staple pets were the canary and the fish.

Living was simple and not complicated with gadgets. There were few major appliances as we know them today. An electric iron pressed the clothing and bedding, and took the flaws out of my father's shirt collars. Washing was over a tub with Fels-Naptha cake soap on a washboard which stood on wooden legs about two feet high with flat metal pressed into ridges that resembled the mini-Venetian blinds in fashion today. A hand-operated eggbeater fluffed the egg whites until they stood in peaks above their bowls and became meringue for the lemon pie.

We had no refrigerator, nor did anyone else we knew. Perhaps they hadn't been invented—ours came years later; but our meat did not spoil. No one got salmonella poisoning. Perhaps it had not been invented, either. There were no "health police" monitoring our food. We had iceboxes and an iceman who sold huge blocks of ice from his wagon in the alley. He would look up from the alley at the kitchen and pantry windows where tenants would have placed a large cardboard sign that told what size ice block was wanted. Ice sizes came in 25, 50, and 100 lb blocks. One would order according to the size of the icebox or the size of the pocketbook.

The bare floors in my house were swept with a broom made of real wicker straws—no plastic phony-baloney get-up. An individual straw would regularly be plucked from its place on the broom and be used to test the readiness of a cake baking in the oven. If the straw came out dry, the cake was done. If batter clung to the straw, back in the oven went the cake and we kids would just have to wait it out.

Another kind of sweeper was used for the rugs. It was called a carpet sweeper, though we had no carpet, only rugs. Its bristles, hidden under a metal cover, were fixed onto small wheels and log-shaped devices that looked like today's hair rollers. The carpet sweeper had a long handle and when you pushed it, it rolled over the rugs collecting dirt effortlessly, powered by human hands. The eight-pound "Oreck Man" had not been born.

Our furniture was unremarkable. We had enough of it--not broken down and somewhat attractive. It was not designer furniture.

*My mother - Della Lyons Green, 1926,
pregnant with my brother, Earl.*

Designers hadn't been born yet either, and had they been around they would have starved to death for lack of business. Living room furniture tended to come in sets; a couch and two matching chairs was a living room set. Bedrooms varied. Bunk beds hadn't become popular so single beds, called "twin beds," were used in rooms where children slept. Adult beds were bigger, but were just one size intended to hold two people. There was no such thing as "Double," "Queen," and "King" sizes.

* * *

The most fun I can remember about sleeping was when my brother and I slept on a screened porch at the rear of another apartment we lived in when I was a bit older. The windows were French doors that opened onto a large backyard. We could read late into the night or play games by the light from the alley. When that light wasn't enough, we always had our trusty flashlights as back-up. On very cold nights, Mother put outdoor clothing on us—sweaters, jackets, and scarves, and sometimes a skating cap—to wear to bed. She would pile the covers, sometimes adding a throw rug on top. The whole thing was a ceremony and we felt like we were camping out.

Having fun was mostly listening to the radio, reading the Funny Papers, playing Monopoly indoors. Outdoors we skated and in the summer looked high and low for sidewalks as smooth as the ice we skated on in winter. Once a year we went on a trip to Riverview Park. Belmont and Western Avenues seemed to be a city away from 57th and Indiana where we lived. The rides were 2 and 3 cents; the most expensive was a dime.

After returning from a trip to Riverview, in the middle of the night I heard my mother saying to my father, "Steve, you mean you spent

$8 today at Riverview! How could you?" That was a small fortune in the 1930s.

Daddy walked with me down cold winter streets smoking his cigarettes, which I thought were keeping him warm, and wished that I too could smoke a cigarette. He let me ride in his truck on Saturdays when he would deliver his valet supplies. He carved the Thanksgiving turkey, poured the wine, and toasted the cooks—my mother and sisters. Then one day, all of a sudden, he was gone and at the junction of my life when I would begin two passages: beginning menstruation and graduation. How did he just disappear?

1934

On a hot July night in 1934, my bed was narrow and the bottom sheet was damp. There was no top sheet. The streetlight shone into the room with a glare that seemed to add heat to the already unbearable temperature. I lay there, unable to sleep, watching the swarm of insects around the globe of the street lamp. Then I heard the voices, my mother's first.

> "I will not go on this way. Night after night, it's the same. Why don't you just leave? You've become a tramp. The children need…"

I covered my ears. I did not want to hear her talk about this.

> "Why don't you go to your mother's?"

> "Why would I do that?"

He sang his drunken song:

> *"In some secluded rendezvous…that overlooks the avenue…"*

> "Stop that! I can't stand that song. I'm ready to quit. Let us end this hell before something really bad happens. I want you to leave. I cannot leave; I have the children."

My small body, damp with the heat, stiffened as though frozen. Daddy leave? What would we do? What would Mother do? What to tell Steve, Jr.? What about Joy? Steve, who always slept like the dead, heard none of this. Joy, the baby, didn't even know Daddy.

She was always in bed and fast asleep when he would come home drunk…"And cocktails for two…"

My mind jumped out of that sticky bed and orbited past the light bugs and into the wonderland of life with Daddy before this night. Daddy had always been a mild man. His frown alone or a small gesture signaling displeasure was enough to make us children anxious. He never whipped us but the leather strap for sharpening his straight razor maintained a dominant place on a hook in the bathroom and was forever a threat. Twice he frightened me outright, which may have been the onset of my gender crisis.

Once was on a Thanksgiving Day, when we were walking through Washington Park, picking wildflowers and blowing the cottonseeds—really just killing time until the turkey was done. He shouted to me in a harsh tone: "Stop walking like a boy!" The shock sent urine trickling down my thighs. The second time was when he came to my bed to cover me up and kiss me goodnight. I was scarcely 10 years old. He jerked back the covers and said, "Move your hands." He thought I had been masturbating.

As a very young child, I once went with him to the barbershop. When the barber lowered the chair to shave his face and I saw him lying back in the chair with all that white, foamy lotion covering him and his eyes shut tight, I cried out in fright because I thought he was dead.

* * *

By November of 1934, my parents had separated. Daddy had become a real drunk.

He roamed the streets and hustled drinks in the local tavern. He appeared on the doorsteps of my friends' parents. He was a stranger to his children. My brother told his friends that he was dead. My resourceful grandparents ultimately placed him in a facility for recovery in far away Virginia. As far as we were concerned, he might as well have been dead. He would not resurface until years later when I was a grown woman. As a recovered man, he more resembled a child—meek, humbled, and compliant, living in the basement of his parents' sixteen-room mansion. A forty-something child!

Mother met the challenge of single-parenting for her "three little urchins," ages 12, 9, and 4. We received "Emergency Relief" for less than one year, and she used the service exactly as it was—relief from an emergency. Never did she submit to the welfare culture; in fact, there was no welfare culture in that day. Mother worked on a WPA project, took a Civil Service Exam for work with the Illinois Department of Unemployment Compensation, passed it and was miraculously called to work on the very day her work on the project ended.

I received a telegram from her at Fisk University where I was in attendance on a scholarship. She was so excited she could not use the ordinary mail. It was January 1941. She was thirty-nine years old. The telegram carried the good news of her new job and the salary--$100.00 a month. We would all now be starting a new life. We were once again a respectable family.

1946-1960: Marriage - The Beginning & the End

"Girl, I wish my husband would do that," Regina said longingly as she gazed at the gleaming squares of tile Leo had just finished installing on the hallway floor of our Hyde Park apartment. "And he just takes such pride in it. You are so lucky."

"Your husband is an attorney. I wish Leo had a profession. He is good with his hands but he's not interested in formal education. He finally enrolled in that technical college on 20th and Michigan for a television technician course but I tried desperately to get him to attend a four-year university, go for an engineering degree, which could have included television studies as well, but he wouldn't hear of that. He refuses to see the big picture and he has so much natural talent, he can fix anything. He could make most things."

"Well, he's so good looking, and he's nice, too. Maybe he'll find something later on he really wants to study," says Regina.

Handsome and suave, Leo was the sort of easygoing fellow who didn't mind putting on a tuxedo, loved to dance, and who worked hard, and hung around gas stations shooting the breeze.

The youngest of six children, he lost both parents to death when he was only eighteen years old. Older siblings guided his late teen and early adult years. He was the least educated of the litter that boasted musicians, entrepreneurs, civil servants and one sibling whose name became a household word as he rose to unprecedented heights as an educator. The black sheep of the family married me when he was 25—a late age for 1945 marriages! We had met only six months before when I was out on the town celebrating my graduation from college with a classmate and her date. We were introduced.

"Did you get my name? It's Simeon, Leo Simeon."

"Yes, I got it."

"I bet you can't spell it."

"S-I-M-E-O-N," I blurted back.

"Hey, you must be a college graduate!"

My friends turned to him.

"She is, as of only a few nights ago."

"You mind if I have your telephone number?" he asked.

* * *

Our courtship was romantic and intense. One evening after a movie, we were sitting on the steps in the hallway of my mother's apartment building. I had decided to "confess" my previous involvement with an older woman reputed to be a lesbian. After all, it was knowledge of this that had abruptly ended my engagement to my childhood sweetheart, Hilton. He had been unable to handle such information.

"I know it's late, too late to wake up the folks, so let's just sit here," he said. "I'm not ready to let you go. I keep telling you I won't get any rest until we're married."

Leo falls back on his elbows and pulls me down on his chest. What beautifully wavy hair he has, I am thinking. Marrying him should produce some gorgeous children. That is, if I have any.

I'm always planning.

Leo wants to neck, really neck. It's a perfect spot, but if we begin that, I'll never get what I want to say said. And if I don't tell him now, I may lose my nerve.

I do a pull-up maneuver off his chest, bracing my back on the other wall and clasping my hands around my knees as if I needed to lock my legs closed in order to get on with my serious talk.

"Leo, please pay attention. It's hard enough for me to tell you this. But I have to. It could make a difference. You might not want to marry me."

Leo stops. That got his attention! He knits his brow. That brow which is higher than the other is really arched now!

"What do you mean? Not want to marry you? Did you kill somebody?" he asks.

"Oh no, it's worse than that. I've been going around with an older woman who has a terrible reputation and a closet full of scandals. She's married to a very important man, but people think of her as a slut. But, more to the point, she's supposed to be one of those 'women lovers.'"

I steal a sideways glance at him to see his reaction.

"I met Lil on the job I had with the Treasury Department. You know, where I worked full time while I was going to Loyola. I became smitten with her. She was so outrageous, she was attractive to me. It was an adventure to be in her company. Then there was her husband, Lucius Harper. You've heard of him, I know. He's the editor of the Chicago Defender, Oberlin graduate, also Harvard Journalism. I never could resist important people. Especially if they also had brains, and boy, does he have brains! I became their shadow, their mascot. They took me everywhere. And the nightlife! Their street friends were mostly entertainers, artists, writers—those kinds. They knew I was a student and never bothered m--in fact, they protected me.

"They used to call me "The Book" because I was always carrying one. I'm talking about people who owned taverns and nightclubs and put on cabaret shows. That was a whole new world for me, and I ate it up. It was fun to go anywhere with the Harpers. As soon as they would walk into a place, everyone would roll out the red carpet. When a headwaiter said they had no tables, it was because he didn't know who they were. Then the owner would appear and set up a table in front of all the other tables in the place, and we would prance down to the front, right under the stage.

"But that's not really what I want to tell you about. I want to tell you about this woman and all the trouble this relationship caused. Why, once my mother put me out of the house because she caught me talking on the phone to her after she had told me not to have any contact with her. I even went to live with my aunt until we had a conference, and everyone agreed that Mother should let me come back home. I was only 19.

"Besides that, you know that I was engaged to be married to another person before I met you. He was my childhood sweetheart. He went into the army, and one day he sent me an engagement ring. Well, that's not important either, except that while he was overseas, his mother and I used to go to a lot of social stuff together. We got pretty close. She remarried while her son was in the service, and I was in the wedding. She was so close to me that she could spy on me. In fact, she found out about my friendship with Lil and when my fiancé, her son, came home from the war, he broke the engagement. Leo, are you listening?"

"Of course I'm listening. But something strange is happening to me. Feel here."

He places my hand between his legs, and what I feel is a broom handle.

"I can't explain it. I'm horny as hell. What time is it?"

"Ten minutes to three," I reply.

"You know the traffic in and out of this building has stopped for the night. Your mother only has two neighbors, the old lady on the first floor and she's in bed forever, and on the second floor the family has two kids, and I know they're all asleep."

I'm relieved that Leo has so far handled my story without panicking. I don't even resist the sexual arousal, although I am not sharing it.

"What's all this you're saying about my mother's neighbors?"

He doesn't answer. He takes off his jacket and makes me a pillow. Ever so gently, he lowers my panties without undressing me. The bulge in his fly persists, yet he does not attempt any relief, not even to open the zipper. It is as though he enjoys the delicious pain, the source of which remains a mystery. It is the story I told him. It certainly wasn't an erotic one. What had caused him to be so on fire? I decide to quit thinking about it and enjoy whatever he is about to produce. After all, Leo is a man, and the stairs are, indeed, thickly carpeted. I had to agree. Everyone in this building is asleep, including my mother, who is just on the other side of two oak doors—the hall door where the makeshift pillow rests and her bedroom door.

Leo's wet mouth is massaging my thighs, and that beautiful, black, wavy hair mingles with the thin strands of mine he has exposed. No man had ever! Men before him had hurt me as they tried to relieve themselves—the one or two experiences I knew—but not this. He is still not relieved. The broomstick has swelled to feel like a baseball bat. It is poised against my ankle, and as his massage turns to the inner worlds of my center and my breathing becomes involuntary, I knew, in a way, he was relieved.

> "I heard every word of your story, Shirley. It doesn't really matter what you did before. Now is our time; in fact, right now."

I can no longer stand that huge bulge. I undo him and then "do" him.

He never mentioned Lil Harper again. He also never let me forget our special brand of lovemaking that began that night in the "confessional." And years later, after we were married and he asked

Shirley and Leo on their Wedding Day

for a repeat, his phrase was always, "Do you think I could have some dessert tonight?"

* * *

As the old saying goes, he's a "good catch"—handsome, from a family of credits and excited about being married to an educated woman. I, of course, was open to the idea of a new relationship, having been dumped by my soldier fiancé and betrayed by his mother, my friend.

And so our courtship was brief and intense, and it totally healed my wounded ego. It was emotionally charged with heavy petting, yet no full-blown sex—another irony. I remember a motor trip in 1945 to the Indy Races with the couple who had introduced us. We sat in the back of the car and smooched and petted, arousing each other without interruption for two hours. It was a miracle that this behavior did not result in coitus and pregnancy. We married at the end of six months. No baby for two years. My Catholic mother in her infinite wisdom realized that we were in no position to have children and marched me to one of the first clinics that Planned Parenthood established in Chicago. Catholic, but practical, that mother of mine!

The marriage was replete with instability and adjustments, many of which just went with the times—post World War II era, housing shortages and employment changes. We were constantly moving and changing jobs. Through it all, Leo remained hard working, both around the house as well as for employers. He took great pride in home improvements and I was the envy of all my friends.

Husbands wore suits and ties, attended Graduate School and interned as medics, but wouldn't even pick up behind themselves, let alone tile a floor or paper a wall. Some of our most erotic moments were when Leo was high on a ladder wearing jeans that were tight and puckered at the groin, making the bulge between his legs prominent (predating Calvin Klein's ads for briefs). Often he would put down the paintbrush and we would enjoy unplanned, unscheduled sex in the middle of the day. I remember later, a letter he had written to me dated September 10, 1946, and how sweet it was:

My Darling Wife,

The last twenty-six days have been the happiest days of my life. I may seem mean sometimes, but believe me I don't mean to be.

I think of you constantly at work and at other times too. And as I put the years together so they will work perfectly, I think of how we have been smoothing and fitting our lives together so that we will blend perfectly for the rest of time. Darling, I know that's a helluva comparison but that is the way I think at work.

At home, I think of how nice it is to have you within arms' reach so when I feel like it I can hold you and kiss you. <u>Most of all, I never will have to kiss you goodnight and go home.</u>

Even though I don't tell you every minute or hour that I love you, you should know that I do. For I really do. AND HOW! If I could only find the words to say how much I love you then I could count all the birds and all the stars above you. If only I could be a poet and tell you of your charms, but I'm not and I know it. If I could do all those things, I would do them all for you, but regardless of would or could, I do, and always will, love you.

Your loving Husband,
Leo

But before that, there were problems of great magnitude.

* * *

It is true, one must be careful of one's instincts, especially those that lead to control of others, even husbands. While I was willing to live with the "blue-collar man," I determined that he would opt for the highest paying and most unique of the blue-collar jobs. Believe it or not, driving or even merely riding in a beer delivery truck in 1949 was a rare and prestigious employment for a black man.

In my inimitable way, I persuaded a powerful friend of mine to intercede for Leo to obtain employment with a beer company. I would come to rue the day!

He was hired and our entire life eroded into a never-ending climate of nagging, complaining, anxious me and a defiant, resistant, passive-aggressive him. In addition, he was drinking, not a lot, but daily, and with the fellow workers. It was part of the culture. I assessed his drinking not as the beginning of alcoholism, but rather as a weakness of character. "Can't you just say NO," I would harp. "Couldn't you come home just one night without liquor on your breath?"

The naggings increased and he became more resistant to my many suggestions. Then I became pregnant. I didn't resent the pregnancy. Things could not be more problematic; a baby just might give us a boost, I thought. He certainly liked the idea. Our families were very involved with us, and that helped. It was less lonely. Everyone was having this baby, not just me.

Leo took a genuine interest in our son. He bathed, diapered, fed, burped, did whatever was necessary. Truly bonded, as the saying goes today. But there was an eddy in all this. He hated his job, hated the union structure of it. He was abused by the corrupt union policies. It was god-awful, worse than the insurance job. Worse even than that was the continuation of my power brokering; I had not learned from the experience. Now that we were parents, I decided that the best thing that Leo could do would be to try for government employment, most specifically, the U.S. Post Office. A steady paycheck and all that went with it. After all, postal employment was a pretty high grade of work for Negro men in the 40's. It was middle class. My uncle worked there and he led a very upscale life, taking excellent care of his own family and contributing heavily to mine when alcoholism overtook my father. Postal employees of that day formed organizations—civic, religious, and social. The social groups were men's groups, since no women worked in the post office at that time. They were of a fraternal nature, but not of the Greek tradition. The Assembly, The Ambassadors, The Snakes, The Frogs: a notch below what would become the Greeks—The Alphas, Kappas, Sigmas, Omegas--and laying the groundwork as more and more Negroes became college educated.

* * *

Three years passed, and I finally realized that I was not the marrying kind. What a devastating awakening! What should I do? Beg out, promise him any and everything. After all, freedom was what I truly wanted. I was clever enough and ingenious enough to make it on my own without commitments. No child support. That should make it less complicated.

> "I'll keep the kid. I'll manage. You just go and do something wonderful with your life, something that will make our son proud. Don't worry about me."

He did. And three years later, we remarried. Guilt and depression had overwhelmed me. Such a nice man! How could I deprive him of his family? The second marriage was on firmer ground and presented major projects—apartment hunting, furniture shopping, a new beginning and a second pregnancy. This one was not planned and it seriously interfered with my personal project, the pursuit of a graduate degree.

* * *

The second separation from the second marriage did have a reason. It was not just some vague "I want to be me" theme! I had fallen head over heels for a young doctor and clandestineness was wearing me down. Again, what should I do? I decided that this time I would do it for me, give myself a big way out. After all, he had committed a federal crime.

Leo was lobbied into government work as he had been lobbied into the beer trucks as he had been lobbied into a tweed suit with an insurance premium book in his satchel. And he wiggled himself out of each pigeonhole each time with increasing self-destruction. The last wiggle was the most devastating. He was fired from the post office for stealing. What did he steal? Men's toys: electronics, guns, and cameras. What did he do with this loot? Stockpiled it on a closet shelf in our bedroom. Was he a fence? Was he selling? Distributing? None of the above! Leo was one of the most honest people I had ever known. So what did this stealing from the USA mean?

Why does a child steal who doesn't need the things he steals, or a rich lady steal from upscale shops? There are many reasons: attention, rebellion, frustration, love deficits in the case of a child.

Leo probably engaged in this atypical behavior out of frustration and the inability to express himself in other ways. Perhaps he was weary that his life was seemingly not his own; my best guess in looking back is that I was having an affair with a woman, and he did not know how to confront that. After all, in circa 1956, few men were prepared to acknowledge that a very close relationship between their wives and other women meant anything to be threatened by. What a silly notion! As it turned out, there was a very good reason for him to feel threatened. That relationship with a twenty-something lawyer was demanding all my attention, had escalated to feverish heights and subsequently became the impetus for my leaving the marriage.

The housekeeper was stirring oatmeal and frying bacon. Son #1, Roy, was preparing to wolf it down and run to beat the bell. It was a school day. Son #2, Peter, was in his crib. I was dressed for work and about to leave. Leo, who worked the night shift at the post office, had only been home long enough to have his second cup of coffee when a knock came at the door. I opened it for two very official looking men dressed in business suits at eight o'clock in the morning. They had come to search my house and arrest my husband. And they did just that.

There were rows of boxes that had never been opened until the detectives opened them. It was astounding. I didn't have a clue that Leo —the "Honest Abe" of our circle of friends, who would walk back to the supermarket to return a few cents to the clerk who gave him too much change, the devout Catholic, the good dad, the compliant husband—was stockpiling goods and ammunition from the mail. Leo, the thief! No, it couldn't be; it just didn't fit.

Because of his otherwise clear record, and his family status, he was freed on his own recognizance to stand a bench trial a few months later. His federal employment was immediately terminated.

"Leo, you must have been very upset with this marriage and me for you to do such a horrible thing. I may have to admit that we are not a good match. I'll say that I was not good for you. I'll stay in the marriage until after the trial. The attorney says it will help you a lot to be married with two children, one in such a fine school as Parker. In fact, the school the Judge's son attends. Did you know that the Judge who decided your case might be Roy's friend's dad?"

* * *

A family friend was Leo's defense lawyer. Roy's friend's father was the Judge on the bench. Leo received four years' probation.

Soliloquy

To my sons------------- Roy and Peter

I tried to care for you and protect you while at the same time pursuing my own interests: work, study, ideas, creations—a life of the mind. I did not have to try to love you. I did that without effort. You were lovable. Many women of my day didn't have the courage or the strength to try such a multifaceted life as did I. I was lucky to have the two of you turn out so well. You have both built your own lives, and good ones. Now that you both are middle-aged, I can write about mine.

To my dear deceased Mother----------

I wish you could hear me now. I'm OK. I got educated. Got married. Got children. Got mucho friends from all walks of life. I played Bridge like you did. Got old like you did: with dignity. Nothing really awful happened to me. Oh, yes, I also got a career. All those things you feared would not occur—my delving deep down there into the "well of loneliness." Those things that frightened you—that made you say one night in a fit of rage, "I'd rather see you dead," didn't happen, did they? If you were alive today I know you would regret having made such an outlandish utterance. That was the night you listened in on a telephone call between me and my very first woman lover—a WAC, whom you heard say, "I love you." The phrase threw you into a state of panic. People say that phrase to each other all the time nowadays but having those words pass between two women was unacceptable in 1944. Well, that WAC friend left our relationship because she determined that I really wasn't a "lesbian" after she found out that I was going to get married. By the way, that same WAC friend became the first woman dentist to be licensed in the state of California and enjoyed a successful practice for more than 40 years.

I've written this book about people like my WAC friend of the 1940's and myself so that mothers and grandmothers of today won't go off the deep end and want to consider murder for their children should those children decide to take a little trip—let's call it a sexual odyssey into never-never land. I only wish you were hear to read the book.

Part II:
The Women

There were lots of women and I kept telling myself and trying to explain to those who might listen that loving a woman was not just physical, like devouring a piece of meat is physical, or having a healthy sex life is physical. It was emotional—an emotion I could not find with men. Of course, the world had to catalogue such an attraction. The world needs labels in order to find things, keep things straight, and the world could not easily distinguish between the physical and the emotional. People got really confused when you added "social" to the mix. And, for heaven's sake, don't dare touch the subject of the politics of same-sex liaisons.

I liked men, lots of them. I married one twice. I had two offspring; both are men today. How could I _not_ like men? I even enjoyed sex with men if they were patient and gentle and sensuous; in other words, if they were like women in bed. I like to dress men and walk down the street with men and dance with men. Yes, I liked men, but when a woman attracted me, I became obsessed with her. In my youth, I thought it was love, but maybe it was just lust.

While I was lying in the hospital room, I allowed myself to reminisce, and even to wonder if I could again warm up to the women I loved in my youth. How would it be now to encounter them?

Blanche: if I saw you today across a crowded room, would I flirt?

Elaine: if I overheard you talking about a mentally ill person who was your own mother, would I be so intrigued today as to make you my special project? Would I eroticize your edgy, complicated story with all its shadings and contradictions—poor medical student from the inner city ghetto with a "crazy," institutionalized mother and a philandering father with a secret family on the other side of town?

Lucile: I ask myself, would I cry into your pillow today because you invited me to your bed and then refused to have sex, or because you permitted your cat to share the bed? Would I be driven to tell the world I was in your life? That I drive your car? Go on fishing trips with you because I am so proud to be associated with a classy woman of your stature, who sails through high-end society without a single stain or scandal, her lesbian nature well known but never spoken of?

Miss Savage: would you look as good to me as you did in 1938?

Lil: you brazen hussy, would your savvy allure me today so that my mother would suffer pain and embarrassment because I wouldn't let go of you?

* * *

This woman thing long puzzled me. I have wondered about it from many angles, none of which has been heredity vs. environment. I really didn't care whether one was born gay or lesbian, or selected the lifestyle voluntarily. What I did care about was why it was so important to be identified, to be a "card-carrying deviant." Who cares? I would ask my friends. Is it politics? Is it poetic justice? Is it perverted chic? Sylvia knew and understood and I do believe that she would have been one of the women as attractive to me today as she was in 1965.

Sylvia, the least "sexy" of them all—scrawny, but oh-so-brainy and challenging. Our bond was emotional, for she eradicated the physical and nothing was lost. The passion remained, the intensity and the commitment never changed. Yes, Sylvia was it. Even she could not believe the sustained interest we had in each other because, I guess, our affair began with a strong physical attraction and she thought with that gone, we would fade away; but we didn't. Sylvia is proof-positive that my love for women did not have to include the physical acting out.

In my repertoire, who else would still hold my interest?

1938: The English Teacher

I had selected her class secretly since she was reputed to be the most racist teacher in the entire school, and I could not afford to let any one of my friends know that my enrollment in her English class had been voluntary. Her name was Edith Savage—everyone black like me avoided her and so did many whites. It wasn't that she'd ever been known to have abused or blatantly discriminated against a black student; it was just that in 1936 Chicago, a white Southern-bred image teacher in a high school with fewer than three percent black students was assumed to be a racist. She became, in our minds, the stereotype we had created from her profile.

I saw her as a challenge and, besides, I found her rather attractive. About five and a half feet tall and slim, she had high cheekbones, thin lips, and piercing blue eyes—a face with character. She dressed fashionably, not dowdy like the other teachers, she had a snappy haircut, and many of the things she wore were youthful enough to make me wish they belonged to me. I still remember a mulberry-colored woolen shirtwaist dress with box-pleated skirts she wore often, and, of course, I remember she drove an expensive car, a top of the line Buick Sedan. I used to arrive at school early just to see her drive up to the school building and park. I would watch her from a window in an empty classroom as she walked toward the school building, her arms folded around her books and papers, her steps graceful and sure.

It mattered not to me that she was said to hate "niggers." I was determined to meet the challenge and show her a thing or two. I positioned myself in the front row of her class, clean and brushed, with my manners also spotless. I was everything she was not prepared to find in a black student: diligent, intelligent, cultured, and initiating. Then, one day, she introduced the study of the ballad, and after only a short lesson on its verse form, she assigned the class to write one. It would become an assignment that changed me profoundly.

I thought of my subject for the ballad while riding the elevated train home from school. Miss Savage had been building up to the assignment of the ballad by lecturing to the class about 19th century romantic works by Elizabeth Barrett and Robert Browning and others, some of which were ballads, others verse or novels. All of a sudden, the great romance of the 20th century struck me. The Daily News was full of the romance of King Edward the Duke of Windsor, King of Great Britain and Ireland, who abdicated in order to marry Wallis Warfield Simpson, an American divorcee. I had read every word that was in print with the same excitement that other girls were reading "True Confessions." I would write about the "affair."

Always a night person, I wrote that evening at the kitchen table after everyone else in the house was fast asleep. This night I was especially late. It was as though I so looked forward to doing this assignment that I delayed getting started. It was three o'clock in the morning, and my mother was calling from the bedroom that I should turn out the light and get to bed or I would never be able to go to school the next day, which was already that day. By 3:30, I was finished and quite pleased with my project.

After I went to bed, I don't think I slept at all; I just lay there awaiting the morning.

When at long last I arrived at my classroom, I anxiously sat as Miss Savage continued to teach the ballad on deeper levels during the day's lesson. Students were squirming in their seats, many not attending the lesson but instead trying to finish the assignment by writing in their laps and under their desks. When the lesson ended and the bell rang, the homework was collected.

The next night was sleepless as well for me as I wondered how my ballad was received. I worried that Miss Savage may not believe I knew as much as I did about the romance between an English king and an American woman twice divorced. After all, most 15-year-olds were not interested in that topic, and certainly not a 15-year-old black student.

I worried that she might not believe I had actually written the ballad, and those thoughts created nightmares for me. I dreamed of castration from her orbit just when I was beginning to make an impact on her as a really special student.

In the morning I dressed meticulously in anticipation of the day ahead, putting on my brown and yellow hounds tooth blazer, a brown wool skirt, cotton round-collared blouse, and my brand-new brown and white saddle oxfords with ankle length stockings. I felt like a fashion model getting ready for a magazine photo shoot, and I was yet to hear the news that the poem was a good piece of work.

Well, it turned out to be better than a good piece of work. The teacher took me aside as I entered her class and spoke to me.

"Shirley, your ballad is brilliant! Sit down, I'll be right back."

She left the classroom to make a mad dash to the principal's office with my poem in hand. Returning to class, she ordered me to the office. I left the class and went to receive my congratulations.

* * *

My life was never the same after that moment my love for the teacher was requited in unimaginable ways. I was her favorite. I became her "project" as she had originally been my "challenge." The role of "teacher's pet," a commonplace name for the "privileged" student, could not adequately describe the relationship we developed. I reveled in the role and was accepted by other teachers as her special one. Needless to say, I lost all friendships with my peers. I was a "turncoat" and the label "shadow" was given to me for sticking so close to the teacher. I wore the label as a badge of honor, not a term of degradation. Was I exchanging friends for the love and support of my teacher who gave me so much—with so much more to come?

Miss Savage pursued scholarship opportunities for me across the country, taking an active interest in my educational future. She wrote to colleges, obtained catalogues, and followed through on the information she received. She began to include me in her personal life. Hers was the very first Lake Shore Drive apartment I ever visited—1400 North Lake Shore Drive. It is 60 years later and I live in the neighborhood of that apartment and I cannot ever pass it without remembering. In today's world the teacher might well have been accused of child abuse; emotional, not physical.

Miss Savage and the principal, a tall stately looking German (Sophie Theilgaard) with silver hair worn in a mannish cut, built a house together and I was privy to the development of that dream house as each brick was laid and each stone set. The addresses were 6840 and 6844 North Jean Avenue in Chicago: twin townhouses, separate entrances, adjoining walls. Two women building a house together in 1939!

Graduation day came for me on a June night in 1940. I already had been awarded a scholarship by Fisk University in part due to a letter Miss Savage had written to the admissions office on my behalf. It went:

Mr. Harold Smith
Fisk University
Nashville Tennessee

Dear Mr. Smith:

Enclosed is the personal rating sheet for Shirley Green. I would like to add a few observations which may help Shirley to obtain a scholarship to Fisk. I have been her advisor for three years.

She has been a student in my English classes during her four years at Flower. I found her particularly gifted in composition. She has a very definite flair for writing. She is one of the best-read pupils I have, and seems to have a comprehension of literature, which would do credit to a more mature student.

Among the students, Shirley is a leader. She was nominated for Vice President of her class in 3A semester and lost the election by only a few votes.

She is very cooperative with both teachers and classmates. She has a generosity of service, which makes her an asset in any group. For some time she was employed in the school office for N.Y.A. work and we found her honest, willing, and courteous. She has an exceptionally pleasing manner and is able to meet the public.

I have known her for mother for many years. She is a highly intelligent woman. The struggle, which has been to support three children, Shirley being the oldest, has not prevented her from educating her family to enjoy the better things in life.

I do hope that you can see fit to give Shirley a scholarship. I am confident that you would find her the caliber of student which Fisk would like to have. In my opinion, she would be an asset to any school.

Very truly yours,

Edith C. Savage

ADVISOR

The scholarship would pay only for my tuition for one year: one hundred and sixty-eight dollars. Room and board, transportation to and from Nashville, books and all extras would have to come from another source. My mother was a single parent, having lost my father to alcoholism a few years before my graduation. She was working on a WPA project, hoping for Civil Service work after having passed a State of Illinois Civil Service Examination, but at the time of my graduation the other job had not come. Her income was all of $85.00 a month. It was unlikely that my mother could afford the scholarship I had won.

Following the graduation ceremony, Miss Savage met my mother in the hallway of the high school:

> "Mrs. Green, I sincerely hope that Shirley will be able to take this scholarship. I have never known a more deserving student. She is brilliant and she should pursue a career in writing. Perhaps she will be able to obtain work this summer."

In 1940 Chicago graduations were always held on Thursday nights, and the Friday following was not a school day. Only "teacher's pets" returned to the school building to help their favorite teachers clean up and pack things away. Of course I was one who returned to school. After a day of much tension between the teacher and me and packing away many books and papers, I reluctantly began to leave.

Miss Savage followed me to the door of the school. We did not know how we would end. Hugging was not fashionable in that day as it is today. She reached in her purse and pulled out an already written personal check for $200, gave it to me, and said, "Shirley, in case you do not get a job this summer, I want you to have this. I really want you to go to Fisk. Take my check and be in touch with me." She kissed me on the mouth—a lover's kiss. I don't know to this day why I did not faint. I staggered home.

A few days later, I started my summer job. I was working as a messenger for dental laboratories, carrying dentures and partials back and forth from dental offices to the labs. Forty dollars a month!

The summer came and went. She and the principal vacationing in New York City, doing the cultural/theater thing; I, in Chicago, working as a messenger and dreaming about college and of course fantasizing about her. In September I boarded a Jim Crow train from the Polk Street Station at 8th and Dearborn in Chicago to begin my new life in the South. I had never been south before. The adventure of college and campus living distracted me somewhat from thoughts of her, but she was never really out of my mind.

Thinking back to my high school classroom and sometimes wishing I were there…My adjustment to Fisk University was good. I did well in my studies, proving I deserved the academic scholarship. I made friends and began to enjoy campus life. I wrote her often, at least once a month, asking her to write back but never delving into more emotional territory. She answered only one letter.

> "Shirley, you are where you should be. Forget about me. Do your work. You are among the very best of your people. You will probably find a husband there."

I took her advice. No more letters. No more hanging on to the memories of my adolescent love. I really got into the rhythm of my new college life. Years later, I married an auto mechanic who was not only good with his hands but had a big brain. I sent her an invitation. She sent an exquisite wedding gift, a serving tray of Waterford crystal and sterling silver.

* * *

When my marriage ended, I decided to look for her. She should have been "late middle-age"—50-ish. I was "late early adulthood"—32-ish. I found her name in the telephone directory. One night, over the telephone, I told her that we needed to meet, that I knew the best restaurants in Chicago and by this time in my life even felt comfortable eating alone in them. I suggested the Cape Cod Room at the Drake Hotel. She agreed to have dinner with me. I could tell that she was surprised.

On the evening of the dinner, I deliberately arrived 20 minutes ahead of reservation time, waiting in the hotel lobby. I wanted to be the one to greet and welcome her. Just as I had on the day I handed my ballad to her, I dressed in my best. After all, it had been more than 15 years. She arrived, looking as stylish as she had those 15 years before.

> "Shirley, my God. I didn't know I would be this excited about seeing an old pupil! You look fantastic!"

> "So do you!" I said. "I've grown up." I told her that I had married, birthed a son, and divorced while we stood waiting for the maitre'd to escort us to our table. "Now, I'm on a new horizon, a turning point."

I looked at her deeply, searching for the familiar and for changes. She looked wonderful. The same impeccable taste in clothes, blue eyes still as piercing! The kiss she gave me on the day after graduation sixteen years ago as she handed me her check still on my lips.

We ordered drinks, just like two grown-up kids in a special place for a special occasion. We talked about our lives, latest news, and the weather. Our waiter was a charming young man who flirted and joked with us while displaying an excellent knowledge of the courses offered. We followed his recommendations. By the time dinner came, Miss Savage and I had broken through the nervousness and were thoroughly enjoying each other's company. We ate carefully, pacing ourselves, sometimes seeming to play with the food on the plates.

"I've been in many different places and I often seem to see someone who looks like I remember you," I said. "Then my imagination runs away with me and I am right back in that classroom, back to you in 1938."

"Oh Shirley, stop it; you're embarrassing me. Always the writer—do you realize you almost recited a ballad just now? Listen to you: 'Whenever such is in my view, I am immediately brought back to you.'"

The dinner idea had proven successful. It was wonderful to have had a grown up experience with a favorite teacher whom I loved as an adolescent and still loved. We left the Drake Hotel. She literally dived into a waiting cab and I found a chair in the hotel lobby, where I sat trembling, sorting through what I had just experienced.

* * *

Sixteen years later I attended a conference of English teachers at the Hilton Hotel in Chicago. Someone was holding a cocktail glass in the bar and was quipping about English teachers. I listened.

"It's interesting—students always fall in love with their English teachers or their gym teachers. Why is that, I wonder?"

To my amazement, another in the crowd mentioned Edith Savage:

"Well, there was one English teacher who didn't have to fight off her worshipers. She already had her lover and, conveniently, it was the principal of the school." She asked if anyone there remembered Miss Savage and Sophie Theilgaard. "They were an enigma for that day, lesbian lovers in the same school, living together in a fancy apartment on the lake. Did you know they went so far as to build houses together? They built adjoining townhouses on the far northwest side of Chicago. Now that was something for 1938!"

I did then speak up—

"I was one of those students who fell in love with her English teacher. It was Edith Savage. I was 15 years old. She changed my life. I wish I could find her today."

Finally, she said that the principal had died a few years ago, and that Miss Savage was in a Kentucky nursing home. She wasn't sure if it was Lexington or Louisville, but she knew it began with an "L."

My search did not end until I located her. It took a year. I probed retirement and pension records, school personnel records, and every other clue I could think of until I finally determined whether

Lexington or Louisville was her city. As it turned out, neither was right; it was Henderson, Kentucky. I remembered Henderson to be the point on that Jim Crow train I took to Fisk when the change occurred. The change of seating in coaches reserved for Negroes according to Mason-Dixon—Fisk students would have to relocate their seats at Henderson.

I was by now 60 years old and looking pretty good. I traveled to Henderson. I was not afraid of the South, as I would have been at age 15 when Kentucky could be lethal, where no black person would have been given help in locating a white person, where a black pupil interested in an old white teacher who had shaped her life many years before would have been laughed out of the state, if not lynched.

I walked into a room of six patients in a nursing home in Henderson. Not quite a ward, but almost. She was propped up on two pillows with a tray of food in front of her. She had no hair on the dome of her head. The blue eyes I remembered were milky gray. The mouth I yearned to kiss when I was her idolizing pupil was sagging at the corners with some evidence of exaggerated salivation. The arms that embraced me in the high school corridor when I had had a bad day with other teachers were skeletal replicas with replicas of skin just hanging there.

She did not recognize me. As I stood at the threshold of her room, I had to decide whether or not I wanted to present myself. It could have been an embarrassing moment for her to see me. Who was to gain by my presence? Did she really want me to see her in this condition? I took the plunge.

"Edith, this is Shirley? I have looked for you for years and I am so happy to find you. Can I have a hug?"

She looked up quizzically.

"Shirley?"

"Yes, I am Shirley, Shirley from Lucy Flower High School."

She pushed the food tray aside, extended her arms, and simply said, "Shirley!" I leaned over and tried my best to hug her. I kissed her forehead. She said that what she remembered most was the good work I did in school, especially my writing. "You're the one who wrote that wonderful ballad about the Duke of Windsor, aren't you?"

I said, "Yes, that's me." Even though I didn't see my face in a mirror, I could tell I was beaming. That's all I wanted her to remember. I came close to the bed, hugged her frail body again, and held it for a long time. Shortly thereafter I left. I stopped at the nursing station and left my name, address, and phone number, asking to be contacted when there might be any changes in her condition. Dutifully, the nurse made note of my information. Then, she looked up from her desk.

"Did you work for Miss Savage?"

This was Kentucky. Of course a white nurse for a white patient talking to a black visitor had every right to think I had been her domestic servant. Why should I bother to correct her? Suppose I had said, "She was my high school teacher. She made it possible for me to go to college. She changed my life. I have looked for years to find her so I could say goodbye to her?" Why would I say any of those things to a white nurse in a segregated, white nursing home? There was no way she could comprehend.

"Yes, I worked for her many years ago."

Two days later, Edith Savage died.

1942: Lil Harper

She was the Dennis Rodman of her day. In a word, outrageous! She was the scandal of the 1940's on the south side of Chicago when a section of that area was known as Bronzeville and presented a Chicago version of Harlem. The legendary Regal Theatre was in the middle of it. There was also the Palm Tavern—an upscale restaurant and bar was just around the corner and on both sides of the center, north and south, east and west were a dozen or more restaurants, bars, supper clubs—all black owned, whose owners and proprietors all knew her, bowed to her and welcomed her into their establishment at any time of day or night. She was their "Dolly."

She was known for her incomparable flamboyance and yet she was not a beautiful woman. Nice "black ladies" such as my own mother knew her as a "husband thief" because she was alleged to have broken up the marriage of a celebrity journalist, Lucius Harper, and they also knew, or thought they knew, the truth of rumors that encircled her about "liking women"—a very unique charge in that day, especially in Chicago's black community. Words like "lesbianism" and "gay" had not yet entered the vernacular of the society at large and certainly not black Chicago. No one knew those words, especially not I.

It was unfathomable that any "nice black lady" such as my mother, I repeat, would have had a 19-year-old daughter smitten by the likes of Lil Harper as was I. She even boasted blond hair in the 1940's, long before any nice black woman would have dreamed of dying her hair. Yes, she was without doubt the female counterpart to Dennis Rodman. She was Lil Harper.

But there was a fascinating paradox. This woman was not sleeping around, she was not "whoring"; she was married to one of Chicago's leading citizens and one of America's most distinguished journalists who was Editor-in-Chief of Chicago's major black newspaper, *The Chicago Defender*!

Her husband, Lucius Harper, was a formidable personality, six feet tall in a rather bulky body—very light-skinned complexion, straight black hair—and could easily have passed for a white man, an Edward G. Robinson clone. He who wore a cigar so well and with such panache, today's cigar aficionado could have learned many a lesson from him. Lucius was the kind of man for whom cigars were made to be smoked.

He was born in Savannah, Georgia, educated at Oberlin College in the 1920's and carried on a debate through his newspaper in the 1950's column with the infamous racist from Mississippi, Senator Edward Bilbo. Harper's eloquent journalism attracted national attention and when the debate escalated to its highest pitch Senator Bilbo challenged Harper to a duel. The whole thing was high drama and reminded me of "High Noon." Harper accepted the provision that they meet above the Mason-Dixon line.

I do not believe the woman Lil would have held such an attraction for me as she did had she not been married to a man like Lucius. The combination of the two distinctly different people was irresistible for me, and I jumped into their orbit feet first.

I was a 19-year-old college student when Lil and I met, working in the US Treasury Department and attending Loyola University at night. She was like no other person I had ever known—cunning, provocative, and seductive, but what she seduced me into was

<u>not</u> a lesbian life, but a high life of what today's culture is calling empowerment and influence; a street life where I met the movers and shakers of the black world on the south side of Chicago, those who represented the movers and the shakers of Ole Man Daley's world, men and women who admired me as a college student and protected me from the dark side of street life. I never felt safer than when I was with her, except when I was with both of them—her and Lucius. Her friends referred to me as "The Book" because I was perpetually carrying one.

I eroticized the relationship! I eroticized the power and the privileges! Being picked up at 7 a.m. in the morning by a Packard car and driven to work by a man with whom most people had difficulty even getting an interview with. Walking into a nightclub with Lil and Lucius when the house was packed and there were no tables available, and then watching the maitre'd rearrange seating, open up space and lead us to a "newly discovered" table right under the stage. How could a 19 year old not be impressed with such grandiosity? I eroticized the relationship! I couldn't even figure out for myself which one of the two dominated my sexual fantasies.

* * *

I was in love with both of them and for two very different reasons. I was willing to submit to either or both of them separately or together. It was the woman whose bed I climbed into when feeling warm and wanted, and it was wonderful not to have to worry about her husband or hide from him. He never objected—he seemed to understand my emotions as a young thing like an old sage; he never forced himself nor inserted himself into the private episodes I shared with his wife. Occasionally he would look our way, but not as a voyeur. Not masturbating. Not demanding. Just there, enjoying this very unique liaison. Accepting, accommodating, and protecting me from any kind of what we would call today "abuse." How delightful it was, being able to explore my own sexuality in a safe environment.

But the price was high. My mother became violently punitive and finally put me out of her house. For a brief period I sought shelter and comfort in the home of my aunt and uncle and ultimately returned to my mother's house on the condition that I would never, ever again, contact Lil and Lucius Harper.

* * *

I resumed a normal life. Began to date men of my own age and married two years later. My wedding was planned as a royal affair and my mother threatened to break the receiving line should I dare to have invited Lil and Lucius Harper to the ceremony.

As the wedding entourage made its way from the site of the reception, southward to 60th Street, miraculously the wedding car got a red light at the corner of 60th and South Parkway just before it was to turn west toward my mother's house on Michigan and 60th. And there in front of the court building of that infamous corner stood Lil and Lucius Harper. We waved to each other; I from the limousine and they from the sidewalk. It was meant to be. They had seen me on my wedding day against all plans to avoid that. For a moment that has lasted a lifetime, I was distracted from the touch of my new husband's hand on my *peau de soie* knee, and questions began about my life, my loves, and my journey that would take 50 years to answer.

1955: Blanche

The marriage was beginning to bottom out. Again, bad news, especially since it was the second marriage to the same loving, good-natured husband. For years I had been the good wife and the good mother. New housing, decorating, getting excited about a tile floor, upbeat furnishings, having friends in, playing bridge, pleasing relatives—good, clean fun. But I could only play house so long. Then the ache would set in, the gnawing of my gut, like an itch. Soon I felt my identity disappearing in a parade of entertaining, and resented my privacy being invaded. I was neglecting my other half; no, not my spouse half, but my <u>own</u> other half.

To try to boost myself and extend the marriage, I decided to go back to school. I had just been awarded a State of Illinois Mental Health scholarship to a university of my choice, replete with a substantial stipend for living expenses. Quitting my social work job with the County, my husband treated me to a week's vacation with friends in a nearby Michigan resort. It was to be a new beginning.

Not until I stood in the registration line at the University of Chicago Administration Building and spotted that Latin looking Parisian with patent leather hair wearing a camel's hair polo coat, collar upturned in the Dietrich tradition and felt my heart knocking a hole in my chest, did I realize it was more than learning I sought in going back to school. I needed to answer the call from my other half-my lesbian half. In that registration line in October of 1955 a signal from my pounding heart told me that my "other half" just might be the one wearing a polo coat. In line she stood, never once suspecting me of targeting her.

I made the first move.

"What are you registering for?" I dared to ask.

(Openers)

"Social Work Graduate education."

(Closure)

"Me too; I meant what <u>specific</u> courses?"

"I didn't know we had a choice. Aren't they all required courses, the first year?"

(Neutral mode)

"I feel so old among these kids."

(Reopens)

"I know, I do too! I have had another career and going back to school at my age seems a bit perverse."

(Sharing)

"What was your career and how old are you?"

(Probing)

The registration line is moving more quickly now.

"I was a ship's nurse on the Matson Line. I'm 32."

(Sharing)

"That sounds pretty exotic. You left California to go to school in Chicago? How come? I thought nobody ever left California."

(Small challenge, but not yet confrontational.)

"Chicago has the best Social Work school in the country outside Smith College in New England and I didn't think I could deal with the Smith College elitism, so I came here; and by the way, how did you know about the Matson Ship Line?"

(Surprised that a black student in the registration line at U of C in 1955 would be aware of a Pacific Ocean liner.)

"Just like you know about the QE-2," I retorted angrily. "It's out of New York. You live in California and yet I should not, would not, be surprised that you would know about ships of fame no matter what waters they may sail in. Everybody knows about the Queen Elizabeth.

"I keep up with that kind of stuff; it makes it possible for me to talk with strangers in a registration line."

(A small flirtation.)

We registered and our conversation in the line ended.

* * *

A week later when I walked into my first class, I looked for her. There she was; it didn't have to be. Green turtleneck, black skirt, no jewelry, little make-up, and that hair! I did not want to sit next to her—too much, too soon. We both exchanged a "hi" from across a couple of aisles.

"Where do you live?" she asked as we were leaving the classroom.

"Just a block or two up the street."

"I'll give you a lift. It gets dark pretty early these days." It was late October and Chicago was back on Central Standard Time.

"How did you like the class tonight?"

The question jolted me to reality. I was watching her start the car like a real driver starts a car, like it's part of her, not some intimidating machine. She put the key in the ignition without even looking at it, simultaneously taking the steering wheel with her index finger and rolling it back into the up position. Her feet on both brake and accelerator! Nothing she did was what would be considered "girlie." It reminded me of the left handed compliments I had received by people who said, "You're a good driver; you drive like a man." That remark was made before sexist remarks became politically incorrect.

In seconds we were at my front door—an apartment on 55th and University; a huge complex of apartments with many, many doors, a court building as they were described in 1955. My door was in the rear of the court. She let the car run and walked me to my door. I wondered about her protectiveness. Did she see me as needing help? I was sturdy, sure-footed, and I did not know I was pregnant. That revelation would come much later.

"I liked the class. I think I'll really enjoy being a student again after so many years."

"What were you doing in those in-between years?"

"I married, had a child and decided to go back to school."

A pause.

"I appreciate the ride. Maybe one day you'll tell me the answer to the questions you've asked me. Like 'Where do you live and what were you doing in the in-between years—after Ship's Nurse and before entering U of C for graduate education in Social Work.'"

"I'm sure I will. Let's just give it time."

"Okay, goodnight for now."

* * *

After every class session I got a ride home. There was no need to ask each time if I wanted one. One night just before I left her car I said:

"I'd like to ask you to dinner. You've been so wonderful to me, driving me home after class for a whole semester."

We decided on a dinner date. I was going to cook a fabulous meal and introduce her to my personal living space, my son, and my husband. I was going to bring my academic self into my domestic scene and hope the two might merge.

It was perfect; Leo was flattered that I wanted to share a new friend from my new life. He was indeed the genial host. Roy, age 8, was a good boy at dinner, mannerable, conversant, but not dominating, as children are wont to be. They enjoyed being included and they liked her. Leo planted a kiss on my lips and whirled away. Roy went to his room without being told. Homework for him and bed!

"Want a drink?" I offered.

"Fine idea, what do you have?"

"Scotch on the rocks."

"Great, I don't get that often on my budget, and wow, a really good Scotch, I see!"

I poured Cutty Sark over two big ice cubes in two short, fat whiskey sour mugs. I handed her one. She anchored her elbow on the dining room table, creating a pedestal for the glass, resting in on her cheek—a gesture I would come to see and admire a thousand times over; it would continue to hold the same fascination for me as it had that night.

"Blanche, I'm a lesbian, and I haven't quit thinking about you since that first day in line. Does that make you uncomfortable?"

I had blurted it out. It was shocking, raw, almost uncouth, and totally out of context.

She almost jumped out of her skin, and for years afterwards when she would be telling of our first encounter, it was not the registration line she referred to, but the shock of that moment in my living room. For the next 25 years life was never the same for either of us.

* * *

After that night school took on a new dimension. I studied with a passion and made good grades. I became a better wife to Leo, a better mother to Roy. It was 1955, I was three months into my graduate studies, and I was excited about being a student again; I was in love and I was pregnant. A mixed bag of emotions surrounded me—I was also frightened to death that I might be facing expulsion. The Dean of the School of Social Work had already advised me that my days were numbered. Something about needing to be simultaneously enrolled in classes and assigned what was termed in those days as Field Work Placement. That simply meant that the student must adhere to the policies of the agency where they were doing Field Work—a kind of internship—and my assignment was to an agency that did not have women on staff past the fifth month: the Veteran's Administration. A man's social service agency, as it was catalogued. Men were not supposed to be exposed to a pregnant-looking woman. After the fifth month you looked as pregnant as you were.

How could this be? My university. My progressive, liberal, open, tolerant, flexible, beloved university! How could such a place have a Dean in the most human-oriented department—Social Work— a Dean who would dare to suggest that I must have a "character disorder" since I could not make up my mind between family and a career? Did this really happen in the middle of the 20th century?

Blanche was empathetic. Our relationship continued despite my unshapely, non-sexy appearance. Years later she would amuse our friends with tales of our beginnings by telling of the courtship with pregnant me, years later when fate would have miraculously brought us together again after so long of being separated from each other. Those in-between years meant birth and parenting for me and an affair with another woman for her; an affair that crashed.

In the meantime, I was seeing as much of her as I could possibly manage: after class drinks at Jimmy's, quick cafeteria dinners at Billings hospital where she worked at her old profession, stolen moments over coffee and visits in her car. We had middle of the night telephone conversations after she made rounds when I would pose a burning social work question to be explored, the answer to which might produce more learning than homework. Her 3 to 11 shift was best of all for this-- Leo at work, Roy in bed! She was smitten with Freud; I was not. She was the intellectual; I was the pragmatist. Yet I clung to her every word and noticed how she mesmerized others in our class as well.

We would sit in a booth at Jimmy's with a cheap bottle of wine to be shared. I would think this was to be our moment. Then, before I knew it, a crowd would have gathered. Classmates scampering for space in our booth to listen to her pontificate! European flavor, born in Paris, a kind of 20th century de Beauvoire! No one could resist her. I would shrink into the background and silently pout that our privacy was once again eroded. She would reach under the table, caress my thigh for only a moment, and I would be satisfied to wait it out. I had the staying power and ultimately the last drop of wine would be drained and the others, one by one, would leave us to heaven.

A Poem

I planted a flower in rich, dark soil one day,
And tended it with loving care, giving it source and
Resource for living. I watched the flower in beauty
grow.
Then the autumn leaves fell, covering my
Plant from view, and the snows came and
Blanketed the earth. And children's feet pounded
The place where the plant once grew. And
I thought surely my plant was dead.
But in the spring the sun shone bright,
And one day, two blades of green peaked
Their heads above the earth's brown surface
And lifted their heads toward the sun,
And I thought surely, nothing can kill
This flower, for its roots are deep and true.
So like the plant—is my love.

That poem, so descriptive of my life to come, my life with Elaine.

1956: Elaine

The phone rang. An old buddy was calling to see if I would come over to make a fourth at Bridge! "One of the players from our afternoon game has to leave, and we want to continue the game into the evening." I was tickled pink to be invited among people who would not be nursing and comparing inches and pounds and formulas.

My baby was three months old. Having to leave graduate school because of the pregnancy had been painful enough. I needed an evening of conversation and competition with friends. So, in my high fashioned walking shorts, which confirmed a toned body after childbirth, I literally flew out of my apartment and down to the corner of 55th and University to wait for the westbound bus to South Parkway, where I would safely walk a block and a half to 5326 where my Bridge game waited.

Bridge had been a defining part of my life but never so much as this game would predict. The players had taken a break and were talking when I arrived. Val gave me a hug and made a complimentary remark about my flattened stomach. When she introduced me around, she interrupted an older woman at the table who was talking about a friend's husband's mental breakdown and recent institutionalization. Then a very young woman spoke up. Her name was Elaine.

> "My mother has been schizophrenic. Since I was nine years old. I don't see her often because I'm in medical school, miles away. It's that sister of mine who lives in Chicago I expect would visit her but she's afraid. She acts like mother's mental illness is some kind of disease she might catch. My sister's attitude

enrages me. Mother sits out there in Manteno waiting for me to come to town."

The older woman's account of the husband's institutionalization took a back seat to the instant candor of the young woman medic.

Immediately I was focused on the young medical student. The paradox in her story intrigued me; also the courage to put it out there among strangers! I was riveted. A black female medical student with a schizophrenic, institutionalized mother!

The pieces of the puzzle did not fit. My background had presented medical students as members of families whose parents had been doctors, who were clearly of a black intellectual elite—I knew no medical career aspirants who had the background of this person. And there was to be more.

The Bridge game proceeded, but my attention was divided. I became fascinated with Elaine. She was a medical student, candid, and a woman of 21 years with a "crazy" mother. I found myself eroticizing this young person. I was gazing at her and to my delight she was gazing back at me. Neither of us knew why. Let us just call it "chemistry" until the rest of the story evolves.

Val announced that we were playing the last round as she tried to bring the evening to a close. Scores were added and players reached for sweaters and wraps, as the husband of one player who was to be our chauffeur had arrived and was clearly ready to move on.

The young medic was the first to be deposited at her doorstep. An even more dramatic paradox presented itself than the one that caught my attention earlier in the evening, during the Bridge game. Elaine was dropped off in front of a building on 43rd and South Parkway surrounded by shiftless men in tattered clothing leaning on light poles, with their bottles of wine tilted to the sky. She lived upstairs over a street level liquor store. I had never known a friend who lived over a liquor store! The intrigue I had for her escalated, as did the eroticism.

* * *

The events of the evening's Bridge game at Val's house dominated my thoughts the next day, and I could hardly wait to try the number Elaine had given me. It was the number of the University of Illinois laboratory where she had obtained a summer job.

"Do you always answer the phone, or am I just lucky this morning by reaching you so directly?"

"I thought it might be you. I have no idea why, but I did."

I experienced a physical change in my body from the thrill of her response. That made it much easier to go on with the conversation.

"Something very strange happened to me last night at Val's house while we were playing Bridge. I know you are at work and this is not the time to talk about it, but what I am trying to tell you is that I must see you again."

A loud silence hung on the telephone line. Nothing more until later!

A spate of calls followed. The next day and the following days the calls were so continuous and heated, full of double entendre and implication that they could be likened to a whirlpool of passion yearning to pull us both down into its center. Ten days into this dervish of approach/avoidance, I received a call from her in the early morning. She opened the conversation:

"What are you doing?"

"Waiting for you," I replied.

"I don't know what this means, but I love you," she continued. "Do you hear me? I don't use that word every day."

I made a date with her to descend into the vortex.

* * *

Work then called me back to a measure of reality. As a social worker, I went about visiting my clients, a necessary plan for determining continued eligibility for financial assistance from the County.

A few days later when I went to discharge my duties, I stumbled upon the name of my young medical student. It was not at the address where she had been dropped off the night of the Bridge game. "Worth" was not a common name. For a moment, I was stunned. Could there be a connection?

The welfare recipient admitted me, and when I inquired about the name on the doorbell, which was different from the recipient's, she told me:

"Oh, Worth. No, he doesn't live here, but he pays the utility bills; that's why it's necessary for his name to be on the door…"

My curiosity peaked! Could this woman be in any way related to my young medic friend from the Bridge game?

"I have two children by Worth."

"Does Mr. Worth have another family elsewhere that you may know about?"

"Yes, Mr. Worth has a grown daughter in medical school, another daughter who is married and living in Chicago, and a third daughter who is said to be mentally ill, much like the mother—Mr. Worth's first wife is mentally ill and at the Manteno facility."

It was impossible for me to carry out my routine work that day. I had to make immediate contact with Elaine and tell her about this very unusual coincidence.

I moved into acceleration mode. I called her and told her that something had occurred in my work life that related to her, but more to the point it may have made some kind of sense out of our initial attraction to each other. Something mysterious; I needed to see her immediately. We must move up the original date. When could we meet? I really didn't give her a chance to reply. I chose the time and the place and the urgency in my voice caused her to acquiesce without question or protest.

On a city bus I traveled from Hyde Park to the loop to a supper club where Errol Garner was performing. I had reserved a table at the London House, an upscale supper club of that day as the rendezvous where I would tell her the little story I had been holding back. The effect of our meeting the week before last hung on me and haunted my waking hours. I was hoping my story would set the tone for the evenings to follow. I wanted to let her know I could be trusted, that I believed in the possibility of the unexpected. She was waiting at the door of the London House when I spotted her. I noticed that her raincoat was limp and faded from washing; her general appearance was totally inappropriate for the London House. It all excited me more. I would reserve the knowledge of my chance encounter with a member of her family until the right moment in the evening.

We had drinks and an appetizer and then I could wait no longer, my back was to the wall.

> "I know you are wondering why I insisted that we meet tonight. Something—a profound coincidence—happened right after we met at Val's. You remember when I told you about my job and how it takes me into the homes of people receiving assistance through the Social Service Agency where I work?"

> "I remember," she said with a darting movement of the daring brown eyes.

> "The reality is, of course, I'm spying on them as much as rendering service and anyways, I hate that part."

I suddenly felt a little listless and more than a little embarrassed. I tried to stay focused; this story could bond us, or conceivably alienate us since I was describing her family. I had a sudden flash of Elaine bolting up out of the booth and rampaging for the door. So I plunged.

She sat watching me with a scientist's eye, wondering where all this talk was going. I continued.

"You see, a few days after we met I was visiting a new client, a new household on my list. I saw your last name on the doorbell and when I finished asking my usual questions of the welfare recipients, I asked about the name on the bell, which wasn't this woman's own name. She explained to me that Worth was the name of the father of her two children, and though he did not live there he did pay the utility bills which were mailed to her address."

I looked at her over my drink, trying to detect some glimmer of response. She was rigid. I continued to tell her that the woman said that Mr. Worth lived at 43rd and South Parkway, and that he had grown children of his own, one who was "very smart" and, in fact, a medical student.

The largest frown I had ever seen wrapped itself around Elaine. Brilliant young eyes! I had broken a barrier. I tried to recover in a positive way.

"It was incredible to think that I had discovered your half brother and sister and your stepmother the very week of meeting you. Inez, the welfare recipient, even knew that your mother is in Manteno, and she said so with true compassion. I said nothing about knowing you.

"So all this drew me closer to you over the last two weeks. The gods or someone says that we are meant to be."

I stopped and thought how crazy and paternalistic it all sounded. Suddenly, there I was, an older woman, trying to take care of and look out for this young prize. I studied my drink and then Elaine.

She looked at me shocked and helpless.

> "It's all true. I had heard that my father had other children." She fought back tears. "But I wasn't really sure. I have never seen them—haven't seen him in years—and I was afraid to find out. Thank you for telling me this."

Her voice trailed and stopped. She drew a breath that I knew could be heard at the next table.

We left the club and took a taxi to my apartment. We made love all through the night and at dawn she stood at the window waiting for a cab. I stood behind her watching the beginning of a Chicago sunrise. It was five a.m. I felt pain and despair anticipating what her parting words would be.

> "I will never see you again; you know too much about me. We can never be this close again." She wouldn't look at me. "I must put this out of my mind, forever. Now, you know of my problems, and I cannot, must not, add another problem to my life. I'm determined to become a doctor, to have children, and to lead the normal life that is expected in our society."

I wanted to respond, but I resisted. I certainly did not want her to think I had not heard her, understood her. I felt everything she felt. I wanted her to grind out her fears and overcome her angst through the love I knew I was capable of giving her. I was silent. The Yellow Cab gave a honk. We waved to let him know he had come to the right address.

> "Promise me that you will never contact me again. Ever."

On her way out of the apartment she repeated her request.

"Promise?"

I pressed a folded five-dollar bill into her hand. The cab honked again and drowned out my words as I spoke. She fled to the street, taking two steps at a time. I watched, feeling like a thief of time.

That was July of 1956. We did not end that night or that year. Rather, we launched a torrid love affair that brought my marriage to a screeching halt. We bought a house together and lived a decade in a state of denial. She accomplished her goals—professional distinction on unimaginable levels, personal worth and respectability through her own achievements and her marriage.

* * *

There were several indicators that it might not work between us but I refused to pay attention. I had received an official notice that my building was being sold to the University of Chicago and all tenants would need to vacate. She had been living with me by and large ever since my divorce, but as a hospital Resident she continued to have quarters at the hospital; a fringe benefit for medics--the point being, she never had been forced to make a commitment about housing.

Loving the neighborhood as I did, and especially its anchor, the U of C that lent so much prestige to it, I looked only in Hyde Park for new digs. Never did I even consider anywhere else. Within fewer than 500 feet on East 55th Street there was a high-rise building sitting in the middle of the street, very modern façade, replete with doorman. Living there had once been a "someday wish" in the back of my mind. Across 55th, construction had begun on some look-alike row houses next to a huge poster-like sign stuck in the dirt with the price and bargain-basement down payment: "twenty-five thousand/twenty-five hundred".

I grabbed up my teenage son and took him with me to look at the model apartment in the high-rise. He was fascinated by—would you believe—the electric light switches. Alas! The lights at home were operated by chains and strings that hung down from the bulbs in the center of the room. At dinner the conversation went thus:

"Elaine, I have to move. The University has bought this building. I need to know if you're coming along or not. A two bedroom if you are, a one bedroom if you're not. I looked at an apartment today, just down the street—the building is called 'University Apartments.'"

"How much?"

"Three-thirty-five."

"I wouldn't pay that to rent. What about those row houses that are going up across the street?"

"Those are out of the question for me. I can't buy a house. You must be crazy."

"Well, look into it. We just might be able to get one. After all, I'm a doctor and though my income is small now, people always think doctors are going to eventually be rich and even if they are not, they usually welcome them in a new building project like that one seems to be."

From that moment on, visions of sugarplums danced in my head. The thought of owning a brand-new townhome in Hyde Park, and with a female doctor partner—I could set the world on fire. The realization of such would be a super slap in the face to those who opposed same-sex relationships, those who didn't know what or how to think of my relationship with Elaine in the first place, those who worried about the children being raised in such a household with two women. Here were two women defying society by even thinking about buying a house together—both respectable, educated people, one a doctor! Rare in 1960. Well, it happened and the oil and water of our two personalities played out one of the most tragic experiences of my life.

I, the typical Hyde Parker—liberal, progressive, non-conventional, and she—the conservative, closeted, conventional, cautious one-- discovered early on a dramatic clashing of values. Not only was the true nature of our relationship a hidden one at all costs, but the side effects reached into every single aspect of living and, I must sadly add, of my parenting. For example, can you imagine that she objected to my 8-year old wearing gym shoes to school? The house was appointed mainly with my furniture since after all I had had a house before, and a life—a married life. Naturally, my taste and my belongings dominated the house in the beginning. She purchased some furnishings, such as her bedroom set, drapes and carpet. It was a three bedroom house, with one large bedroom the size of the two smaller ones. The large bedroom immediately became hers with a huge king-size bed, while my sons, aged 4 and 12, were relegated to one of the smaller bedrooms and I to the other. This arrangement was so glaringly inappropriate that it called more attention to its effort to disguise the relationship than it would had we been sleeping in each other's arms. Of all the things I am ashamed of in that relationship, the most hurtful was the fact that I permitted such emotional abuse.

* * *

The years in the townhouse rather than nurture and fortify our relationship hammered a nail into proof positive that this could never endure. Some of the nails were tiny thumbs and others were long, piercing nails that went to my core. She did everything to distract from our lesbian image as co-owners of a house, including male lovers, female would-be lovers. All I needed to do was leave. Move. Get back to that apartment building I once wanted. I never was a passionate homeowner. As a young married woman, I resisted the notion of "saving to buy a home of our own," which was my husband's idea. I was indeed an apartment dweller. Land meant little to me. So, why did I not escape? Was I afraid to let the children know I had made a mistake after wooing them into this situation? I wondered then, and I wonder now. It took years of abuse before I one day had the courage to up and go. Maybe that is what it takes for others in these situations, whether with a same-sex partner or a conventional one. It also takes a little help and I got that one fine day when Elaine went on a medical trip to Russia and I discovered myself.

Elaine had been hardworking, determined, and very conservative in her views. She and I were opposites but attracted to each other in a curious way. I had been the seductress. She became addicted and fought the addiction every day of our lives together in one way or another. It was an addicted love. She was in perpetual denial, resisting any hint that our relationship was romantic. I pushed for openness. I was not "in the closet." I was not "out of the closet." For me, there was no closet. I insisted on an open relationship. She acted out the statement she had made to me standing at the window waiting for her cab... "I cannot afford to add another problem to my life." Yes, the relationship was doomed, leaving the door of my heart wide open for Blanche.

On some level I accomplished my goals, too. I was liberated and set free to explore my worlds, but, most importantly, the story of our lives together is told by a poem she wrote me and by the fact that forty years later we are still friends and that kid who was 3 months old on the night we met, and who is now 41 years old, has enjoyed her love and support over his entire life.

1968: Blanche, Part II

Elaine was airborne, en route to a medical meeting in Russia. I had taken her to the airport. When I came home, I let my mind wander for a while. Then I got into a frenzy about cleaning the house. I changed sheets, emptied garbages and cleaned the refrigerator all at once. It was an obvious statement of sweeping Elaine out—at least for two weeks.

That evening I stared at the telephone. My thoughts went in reverse. What was I doing before the night of the Bridge game where I had met Elaine? Oh, yes, I was a mother of three months, expelled from a graduate program. Then I was back in time, at The University of Chicago, standing in a registration line, fixated on a woman with the air of Dietrich and wrapped in a polo coat. Could that have been 11 years ago? My God, I thought, I have had a baby, left my husband, fallen in love with an orphan/medic, and bought a house and am living miserably.

I wondered where in hell the Dietrich-in-a-polo-coat could be tonight. No one would be able to guess, so unpredictable she had been.

I picked up the phone.

> "Operator, do you have a listing for a Blanche Bradley in Chicago?"

God, it's been eleven years. How could I expect to find her?

> "I have three listings…two listed as Blanche Bradleys and one listed as D. Bradley."

"I'll take all three numbers down…"

I picked a number blindly.

"Hello? Hello, could this possibly be the Blanche Bradley who attended the University of Chicago in 1955?"

A second of silence, and then, softly:

"Yes, it's me, Shirley."

And suddenly it was 1955 again.

* * *

But it wasn't all easy. Blanche resisted a meeting at first, claiming a severely depressed state and no interest in social contact. I pushed for a meeting to which she reluctantly agreed. I had no motive other than to see her and enjoy the memories. I wasn't anticipating a romantic rendezvous, or a sexual encounter, no way!

Blanche remembered our affair and the fireworks it represented so much so that she could not handle a repeat.

Our meeting place was at Blanche' apartment on Briar Place. She was wearing a black turtleneck T-shirt, some baggy pants, no shoes, and her patent leather hair was curling at the temples and the neckline, just enough to take the hard edge off her otherwise "lesbian" look.

"Blanche, I am so glad to see you. I can't believe I found you after so many years. Why don't we just relax and talk about old times? Bring me up-to-date on you."

"I tried to tell you on the phone, Shirley, that I'm deeply depressed, and I'm not really good company."

"You don't have to entertain me, Blanche. I don't care if you're good company or not. I just want to revel in the fact that we're in the same room."

"Shirley, we've been in many a room with each other and you know what always happens. You're eleven years older; you've had a baby, but, God! You're more attractive than ever…I've been in a relationship that went sour, and I haven't recovered. How can I tell you about that?"

"Try."

She lifted herself from the seedy couch that was part of "furnished apartments" on the north side of Chicago in the middle sixties, walked inches to the kitchen and pulled out a bottle of cheap Scotch, for which she apologized.

"I can't afford to buy Cutty or Chivas Regal these days. Hope this is okay for a drink or two."

She threw a couple of ice cubes into two glasses, splashed some of the Scotch on top, extracted a few drops of water from the sink faucet and returned to the couch.

"So you want to know about me? Well, have you ever heard of Gregory Cordell?"

"The name's familiar. Isn't he some hotshot at the First National Bank who's making a reputation for himself with ghetto kids—placing them in job training programs the bank is sponsoring?"

"He's that and a lot more. He's doing a lot of international PR for the bank, but the point is he's gay, and he has a sister who moved in on me and my lover of seven years and who has literally taken her away from me, to use an old-fashioned term."

"The sister's also gay?"

"Yep."

Blanche replenished her Scotch. I hadn't touched mine. The conversation was making me drunk.

"So, this is why you're depressed?"

"Shirley, I know you don't believe in depression. Not clinical depression. I remember all those arguments we used to have about Freud and his theories. I know you think all I need to do is distract myself, meet other people, become active, go out to dinner, get involved in life, maybe even have an affair. I know you think I'm nuts, since I'm such a student of Freudian thought. But I tell you there is such a thing as clinical depression, and you don't get over it by becoming active!"

"Blanche, what I thought about Freud in 1955 has nothing to do with today. If you feel you are sick, that concerns me. I don't really care why you feel that way. I want to be involved in your life—sick or well. You were the most powerful force that ever came into my life, and I have not, never will, forget that, no matter what has happened to either of us during the in-between."

"Yes, I know, that's why I didn't want to see you."

I allowed my hand to rest on her knee. It was just a gesture of closeness that went with the moment, nothing more. All of a sudden the room screeched with silence. Neither of us could speak a word.

I made the first move because I felt beckoned. My hands went to the part of her neck just under her earlobes. My fingers pressed as though to steady her head upon her shoulders. I dared to look at her and to force her to look at me.

Her slightly bulging eyes said "Yes" and I planted a gentle kiss upon her top lip. Almost sisterly, if let alone. But she did not leave it alone. She dived into my mouth, opening hers as if to devour me, and within seconds, we were tearing away the clothing that had protected us from our passions without ever leaving the orifices of our bodies.

Today, we could not report where we made love—whether it was on the seedy couch, on the floor, or some other corner of the tiny apartment on Briar Place. We only know it was all-consuming, and while it did not "cure" the clinical depression Blanche held onto for months, it did tell us that no matter who may have impacted our lives before-husband and children on my side, other lovers on hers—we knew that whatever there was that drew us to each other was uniquely our own and had to be attended.

* * *

The next day:

"Hello," from Hyde Park.

"Hello," from Briar Place. "Would you like a cup of coffee?"

"I'd love one."

"Then why don't you come over?" You would have thought she was just next door.

"I'll be right there."

During the weeks of Elaine's Russian trip the juices never ceased to flow between Blanche and me. At first I drove my car blindly day and night to her side of town, then it seemed as if the car just drove itself. It had learned the way. We were totally consumed with each other.

We began to plan our move to San Francisco!

When Elaine came back from her medical meeting, I was cheerful and confident—different from what I had been before. That heavy billiard ball of anxiety, which had lain in my gut for eight years during life with the doctor, had vanished. The miracle of a single telephone call, a roulette kind of miracle, had brought Blanche back to me. But the story with Elaine was not quite finished…

The Ride to O'Hare: Elaine and Blanche

I was singing along to myself in anticipation of the next few hours. Dancing about in the house, rather giddy, when she walked in from her trip to Russia. I had heard her key in the door but I thought it was my son. I did not expect her so early. In fact, I had planned to be out of the house en route to meet Blanche who was returning from San Francisco, where she had gone 2 weeks before to pursue employment.

Though surprised, I was not thrown off balance. More relaxed. More confident. More self-assured than ever. Certainly more than I was when she left two weeks ago amidst a flurry of tension and unspoken words. Two weeks ago seemed like two years, so much had happened since that infamous day when Elaine left for the medical meeting in Russia and I drove her to the airport in an atmosphere of loud, hostile silence, neither of us speaking.

I had returned home that day and started cleaning house—making beds, changing linens, rearranging furniture. I behaved like a madwoman. All I could think of was the hit song from *South Pacific*—"I'm Going to Wash That Man Right Out of My Hair." I was doing the same thing with Elaine. Then I went to spend time with my friend and confidant, Vivian. We sat in her kitchen stringing beans while she listened to me agonize about the relationship I had with the doctor. It was in that setting, on that night, that I made the decision to leave Elaine.

* * *

Having the courage of my convictions, it was easy for me to be giddy when the returning doctor opened the townhouse door. She immediately recognized my changes. No longer was I the wanting, needy, solicitous, complaining partner she remembered. I had a plan. I knew where I was going and it showed.

For now it was simply to the airport to meet Blanche. She was returning home after visiting Berkeley, where she was executing her plan: to return to the west, to seek employment and check on aging parents. She had been in Chicago long enough—Graduate school, a brief but intense affair with a pregnant woman and a seven-year relationship with another woman that crashed. Both of us had a plan. The two plans had yet to intersect.

I got in my car and headed for O'Hare Airport. Little did I know I was being followed.

Yes, it was true. My rearview mirror confirmed the fact. It was the doctor tailgating me from Hyde Park. All the way to O'Hare and there was nothing, absolutely nothing, I could do about it except just let the trip play itself out as it happened. We both ended at the door of the high-end dining venue The Seven Continents, a restaurant long gone. At a table near a window I could see Blanche in waiting, so to speak. Elaine and I entered the restaurant together and she said, "I knew that was the one," and pointed to the woman at the window.

I went to greet Blanche and told her of the saga. With her usual style and grace, her Parisian elegance holding fort, she simply suggested that I go and bring the doctor to our table.

"She should join us. It's the civilized way."

I did. Moments later the three of us sat and listened to Blanche telling of our long history of days gone by. Our University of Chicago common experience. Our affair and the humor of it since I had been pregnant. She made it sound like a charming fairy tale rather than the Shakespearean comic-tragedy that it was.

Elaine finally left the restaurant. Blanche and I played with the food on our plates and I listened to her tell about her trip. The lovemaking that followed in her Briar Place apartment sealed our relationship forever, though we did not know how our mutual plans would intersect.

At daybreak I headed for home. The sun was truly rising and as I drove south on the outer drive, and its brightness seemed to be celebrating our love. Always did I pay attention to the three main structures ahead and particularly so this morning. There was the Drake Hotel, the oldest and lowest of the three. Then the old Palmolive Building which had become the home of Hugh Hefner's Playboy Enterprises. Rising above these two was the Hancock. The trio reminded me of a picture my mother had made of her three children: me, the oldest and tallest; my brother, in the middle; and my sister, a runt in Easter togs. We called it the "stair-steps."

* * *

I'm driving along, basking in the dawn of my new awakening: the realization that Blanche of years ago when we were both students and I was pregnant had been indelibly stamped in my being, and nothing had changed except the calendar. Together we were like something organic, natural, meant to be. Then I pulled off the drive at the South Shore exit (which in that day was 55th Street) and my car found its way to the third townhouse exit from Walgreens. It had traversed that road so many times, but not for much longer. I rather creepingly entered and to my amazement found Elaine brandishing a kitchen carving knife. I couldn't believe my eyes. She had selected her weapon and that was it.

Elaine the pediatrician; Elaine the first female Chief Resident at Cook County Hospital; Elaine, female and black, a stunning combination for 1959 racist Chicago. Elaine the graduate of that prissy school founded by Rockefeller where all the girls crossed their legs at the ankles, and everyone attended Chapel—Sister's Chapel, nonetheless. Is this knife-wielding person who appeared at the door of the townhouse a stranger, or is she truly the ghetto person I first tried to elevate from the likes of 43rd and South Parkway, the over-the-liquor-store resident with a schizophrenic mother institutionalized at Manteno and a dandy for a father, with a second family replete with children by a woman of no repute?

I did not know how to read her. I pleaded for her not to do anything foolish. I reminded her that my son—age 10—was sleeping upstairs and whatever happened at O'Hare should not have to scare him. With weapon in place, she ordered me to the basement of the townhouse. There we had a street fight, something totally unfamiliar to me, given my conservative, upper-class black Catholic upbringing in which my mother would not even allow me to play with children from certain neighborhoods.

In the basement of the townhouse she actually fought with me, knocking me to the floor and injuring a hip that would later show up as a major problem. Years later I submitted to a psychology treatment involving hypnosis in an attempt to recall just how that hip was broken. I never told her about it, yet she knew that the problem existed. For a time I wore a shoe with a raised lift, and there were several other remedies. I was living in San Francisco and few if any of my family or friends were able to connect the dots and trace back to the fight in the townhouse basement for any answers to a condition no one seemed to be able to explain. In my California life I just had a hip that had degenerated—the diagnosis was osteoarthritis, a joint disorder that is non-life threatening. I left it alone until the pain became unbearable and after a while I submitted to joint replacement surgery. Mine was highly successful, but I never informed the doctor that the fight in our basement had started it all. I would have been too embarrassed to let the California doctor know that I had once been with a woman who fought me and broke my hip.

1965: Sylvia, My Soul Mate

The country was still in mourning over the assassination of JFK two years before. The country was also dizzy with LBJ, a reputed scoundrel from Texas who was miraculously driving legislation through Congress at breakneck speed—legislation that would become the structure of the federal social services as we know them today. He was indeed formidable in his ability to do that and to this day is unequaled. Johnson's great administrative ability and low ethical standards may have given us a new formula for "success." We may need to recognize and taken into account the equation that great administrative ability and low ethical standards often go hand in hand. There is much history to support that equation. Chicago's political history clearly supports it.

But I am not writing about our country, or LBJ, or ethical equations. I am writing about women who impacted my life, women who fell in love with me because we shared a passion for an idea that would evolve into a project and become a tour de force for our relationship. I am writing about women I fell in love with for the same reasons, most of whom were not "lesbian" women.

Without LBJ in the White House in 1965 and Richard J., "Da Mare," in Chicago, there might never have been a piece of legislation named the Economic Opportunity Act, nor a Chicago program entitled "The War on Poverty." And I would never have known a woman named Sylvia.

* * *

Sylvia and I met when Mayor Daley convened a major event at the Sherman Hotel to announce Chicago's Planning Grant and launch

Chicago's "War on Poverty." I was to be the Keynoter. I had written my speech but I needed a typist and editor: a critic, mentor, collaborator. I turned to the source I always turn to when in need, the University of Chicago. Walter Congreve, Principal of the Lab School at the U of C heard my plea, but was not encouraging.

> "The best of all people is the secretary here who just left. She's on vacation now but when she returns, she'll be going to work in the law school."

> "Did she work for you?"

> "She worked for all of us here...Actually, we worked for her. She was terrific. You can't really describe her as a secretary. She was our 'academic mother,' our think tank and our chief critic all rolled into one!"

> "If you would give me her number, I'll call her on my own...I'm a grad student here now..."

> "I don't think she'll do it. She's got a son returning from Vietnam, and she expects to use her vacation to be with him. I wouldn't want you to count on her but she is the best."

I made the call.

> "I'm a grad student at Chicago. I need a typist who can edit, critique, and collaborate with me on a speech I have written for a program the Mayor is putting on next month. It's a big deal event. I need a special kind of typist; in fact, typing is the least important part. Walter Congreve at the Lab School told me that you would be the perfect person but you were not available. He

said your son was coming home from the war, and you were on vacation. I pushed him to give me your phone number, and I promised him that I would take full responsibility for the contact…that he would not in any way be implicated…"

I rattled on, not drawing a breath, not giving her an opening to question.

"By the way, the speech has nothing to do with me as a grad student. I just mentioned that to get your attention. I know how much you love U of C. May I come to your house tomorrow so we can talk about this? There is some urgency."

She was awestruck. It was my direct manner, my candor, that attracted her and the confidence that I displayed that won her over almost instantly—something she told me years later when we would reminisce about our beginnings.

A scrawny little woman with a long crooked nose, too big for her face but not big enough for her curious mind, Sylvia pursed her lips and fixed her eyes on me as though she were seeing some strange species and listened to my story. We were standing in her living room. As she gestured with her proverbial cigarette between her fingers, there were moments when I feared her slightly bowed legs would not hold up her body. It swayed with excitement at the novelty of this encounter.

The work began immediately. She returned to her old office in the Lab School with Congreve's approval and used her own equipment to pound out the words of my speech, often alone and after hours, even into the middle of the night. The end product was impressive, better than good. "Da Mare" loved it. I had earned my place in the sun, and I became a significant player in Chicago's war game against poverty.

* * *

Sylvia refused pay, but I was determined. I had probed around until I learned about salaries in her category at the university, starting with querying her former boss, Walter Congreve, and added ten percent to her basic. I wrote a personal check. That was the beginning of the end.

Removing her glasses with one hand and waving a cigarette with the other she told me I could not pay her.

"Didn't you know this was a labor of love?"

She tore my check into tiny pieces. I had to find a way to thank her. A special evening was planned and detailed descriptions filled our telephone conversations. Anticipation and intrigue raised the emotional ante to a near boiling point. There was another way to thank her and many of my readers may think that this is it.

At a window table in a Michigan Avenue restaurant looking out over the lakefront expanse in Chicago, 1968, of treasured museums, Sylvia looked up at the waiter, as he offered her another drink.

"Would you care for another Rob Roy, Madame?"

I intervened.

"Have another if you wish, Sylvia, but don't get drunk," I said. "I want you totally alert tonight."

"I've been drunk all day with anticipation."

The waiter pretended not to hear.

"Yes, sir, I'll have another Rob Roy."

Hours later, in a tiny room of the hotel above the restaurant, I held her and breathed with her and touched her in places she had never been touched. I convinced her that her body was not the ugly thing she thought it to be as she tried to hide from the light in the room.

Her skin, she told me, was loose and folded in the wrong places. The way she said the words could have provided comic relief for a tense moment, but this was not the time for comedy. I made no response but instead simply stretched and smoothed the skin, handling it as one would handle fine cloth that had been unattended and left in an attic.

And Sylvia had been unattended for a lifetime. I showed her that her loins, which had produced four children, could also produce joy for herself. The bowed legs, of which she was perpetually ashamed, became arches of access and took on a different meaning for her.

A season of rendezvous and passionate encounters followed. Hiding under trees and in driveways with the kids! Two fully grown mature women with college age children! Conversations at three o'clock in the morning, sitting in my car! Picking her up from work, grabbing a sandwich at Morry's Deli on 53rd and Kimbark, then off again to revel in the sheer joy of togetherness. We had found in each other our soul mates.

A beauty shop appointment could become a "date." A coffee shop, the "point" in Hyde Park's shoreline! Any venue would do. But always there was a project in the process. With the speech done I was now working on my Master's thesis and again she was working with me, loving the work, loving me. I was so lucky!

"You make me feel 20 years old and I'm forty-plus! How can you do that?" she would quip.

We made love everywhere and often without ever touching, without any physical contact. "How could we do that?" I would ask her.

With her inimitable ability to put an intellectual spin on just about anything, she had the last word.

"Because some of the best sex takes place outside of a bed."

Then we went on to prove it. Physical sex was suddenly, but finally, cancelled by Sylvia, who thought at the time that she was canceling our entire relationship.

"Shirley," she announced, "I am besieged with guilt. It is overwhelming. It is consuming me. We must stop."

"What, pray tell, has happened to you?"

"A favorite professor at the U of C committed suicide last week because of his homosexual agony. That tragedy brought home to me the scary danger of what we've been doing, and I must admit I too am panicked."

"Sylvia, I can't believe you're saying this. It was you who told me that the best sex occurs outside the bedroom. How could you suddenly decide that our relationship is based solely on physical intimacy? It is not—never has been."

She recoiled; I asserted.

"We will go on but predictably in a different way, but I am not going to accept your 'panic state' and put an end to us, our friendship, and our relationship. No way."

We were no longer clandestine. We could only satisfy our desires to be together by broadening our stroke. Our private world was opened to family and friends—no, no, I don't mean we exposed the intimacy; there was no talk in that day about closets, in or out of them. We had no need to confess. We just enriched others and ourselves by including them. We also increased our time together—a nice fringe benefit.

I got to know the son from Vietnam. She got to know my children. I got to know her stoic husband, the PhD chemist who had disappointed her in marriage. She got to know my mother. We did ordinary things together and many extraordinary things.

Parties, travel, Bridge (her favorite pastime and quickly becoming mine)—she was a Master, I, a Novice. I am still a Novice after 50 years of play.

What makes an affair come to a screeching halt? We never again participated in physical expressions of love and intimacy. What makes love, love, never ended.

Twenty-five years later, at her memorial service in the elegant Bond Chapel of the University of Chicago, I participated, the only non-relative to have a speaking role in the service. The greatest legal minds in the country that began their careers at Chicago and were nurtured and mentored by Sylvia were in attendance. From Berkeley to Yale, they came, criss-crossing the country with only hours to spare but compelled to be there to say their last good-byes.

Her eulogy annotated her birth, her marriage, and her successful parenting. Her sons were there to grieve their mother, one career military man of high rank, the other a successful San Francisco attorney. Included in my remarks when I was called on to speak were references to our arguments about my work and my hobby. She hated the topics of my academic projects yet she worked diligently with me to perfect them.

> "You'll never be a writer," she once said about my work.

> "You'll never be a Bridge player—you don't have enough of the killer instinct in you."

These anecdotes brought roaring laughter from the mourners.

Ours was a relationship for all seasons. Pray tell, why can't women love each other today without cataloguing themselves? Why must they march down Fifth Avenue with banners? To paraphrase Henry Higgins, why can't women be more like Sylvia and I were?

1968-1979: Blanche

She had been gone since August—gone back to Berkeley. Our "second time around" affair had carried no commitments, no baggage. When I found her depressed on Briar Place in Chicago she had already made up her mind that she would return home where her parents lived and were aging. She had achieved her academic goal for coming east to Chicago to pursue graduate education in Social Work and had suffered through a very disappointing affair, which had ended and left her devastated and depressed. She was so certain of her plan to return to the Bay area that she had already begun to seek professional opportunities there.

Letting me back into her life for a few months during this transition and indulging herself in a love affair with me the second time around was just an interlude. Sort of like tying a ribbon around her Chicago experience—a ribbon that bore the inscription "1955-1968."

So when the telephone rang for me in my mother's house in Chicago on my 45th birthday, I thought it to be a local friend giving me a birthday greeting. I was flanked by a handful of old friends playing Bridge, friends who knew my life was upside down, who knew I had given up what they perceived as an enviable life in a prestigious south side community, who knew that I was temporarily living with my mother but didn't have a clue of the specifics. They had gathered to acknowledge my birthday, and no more than that. We were playing Bridge. Soon we would have ice cream and cake—a ritual in my family.

I answered the telephone call and when I heard Blanche on the line I was overwhelmed.

"Happy birthday. I'm calling you because I have decided I would like to have you join me. I've thought about this seriously ever since I got back and I miss you too much for us to be 2000 miles apart."

I was beyond overwhelmed. She continued!

"I want you to come, visit and spend some time so you can get a feel for the place and see if you could really live there. How about Thanksgiving? That gives you six weeks to think it over. But let me know because I will need to do some fancy foot planning."

All I could say was yes. Yes, yes, I said yes to everything.

It was October. I was in grad school, plodding along slowly toward an M.A. degree. Son #1, Roy, was in Korea. Son #2, Peter, was in eighth grade and was expected to graduate from elementary school the coming June. More to the point, I was homeless, rootless, dangling in the air, living in my car, waiting for life to happen to me. Back at home at middle age and devastated.

Life happened to me. In the next day's mail I received a greeting card from Blanche. A picture of a child, barefooted and with arms flung apart, stood on a beach. The words read, " There's a great big beautiful wide, wide world out there!"

1969: Bernice Wolfson

Nineteen hundred and sixty-nine was a tumultuous year, indeed. I was in love. I was leaving home, my hometown, my family and a long-term relationship with a black female partner—a doctor, no less. I was a student, a scholar, and launching upon academic projects of a feminist and gender related theme. In that context it was thought that since few or no black scholars were interested in those topics, I was also leaving my race. White themes, white research questions were driving my career, which predictably led me to white women, and some white men.

The University of Chicago was my workshop and my playground. A conference on the status of women was convened by a university faculty department head that included me, the only black student invited to participate.

Bernice Wolfson, a visiting professor and a feminist from the University of Wisconsin seemed to set her sights on me. She was studying under the great Philip Jackson, the preeminent authority of that day on childhood education. We immediately connected, and the reality of my plans to give up everything familiar and move west to begin a new life with a white woman intrigued her. She began to eroticize the friendship we were beginning.

This was so unique in her experience that she fell in love with me and with the idea. She lived so vicariously through my plans and my anticipation. My raw, open love for another woman titillated her in a pornographic way, a voyeuristic way—to such an extent that physical expression could not be restrained. I, so full of joy and sexual anticipation, submitted to lovemaking with her, yet never feeling betrayal of the love awaiting me 2000 miles west. Her attentions to me were intensely emotional and physical, and I admit that I was flattered. My encounters with her became a rehearsal for the life ahead.

Years later, lying in the arms of my west coast lover, we played the old game of "who-before-me-and-when"? She admitted having had a one time sexual encounter with a black man on the Oakland Bay Bridge after they had left a conference both had attended in San Francisco. This occurred while committed to me and waiting my arrival. She laughingly said that she thought that since he was black, handsome, and sexy it might be a good orientation for her future life with me, her black partner.

I never told her about Bernice, the Jewish female scholar from Wisconsin, who called me one night from Milwaukee saying she needed me and drove two hours to Chicago to get me and take me back to her apartment—a five-hour and 200-mile effort.

1969-1978: The Good Life

The greatest of all adventures in living was mine for a decade, and it was also the most dangerous, the most turbulent, and the most anxiety producing, yet the most satisfying. I had what few have—a chance to live out my fantasy. To build a traditional family life around the most treacherous and unconventional base and to dare to develop such a life with a teenage child around the world's most hated taboo was indeed the challenge of my life. It wasn't supposed to work.

We moved into a brand-new condominium in a brand-new neighborhood and were able to delight the teenager with his very own dog. Everyone had his own space, with some to spare. Blanche' Berkeley parents became Peter's west coast grandparents and treated me like an in-law. A gift of cookware was given to us by her parents, which could almost claim heirloom status. Each of us had responsible and rewarding jobs: Blanche as a psychotherapist working with the parents of disabled children and I as a grant writer assistant in the Planning and Development department of a prestigious school district. Together we earned enough to maintain a high lifestyle—each with our own automobiles, an interior decorator, handsome wardrobes and enviable entertaining.

Blanche took an interest in Peter's schooling and attended parent-teacher meetings as the good surrogate parent that she was. There were ski trips on weekends, motor trips up and down Highway 101, overnights in Carmel, Monterey, and Big Sur and never did we flinch or apologize for being an unusual "family"—an alternative family as we were called in those days. Nor did we encounter any flinching or questioning from others. Blanche was an amazing person: born in Paris, France, and raised in the Berkeley hills with enough panache and savvy for two people. She found me to be an eager learner about a certain kind of dining, wines, dress, and many other things. I found her to be a superb teacher.

I was educated and had had a considerable amount of exposure before we got together, so I wasn't exactly a dud; I just needed "finishing." I loved modern art and had a nice collection, but I needed to learn how to distinguish between a good piece and a poor piece and to understand what the schools call "art appreciation." I learned from Blanche. I learned how to express myself through household furnishings, wardrobe, and a thousand other things, such as how to carry off mismatched table service and how to combine our two individual personalities in the things we bought and the ways we furnished our home: "old world/nouveau riche," in excellent taste.

* * *

About 1974, Blanche and I were both changing. We sensed it in each other long before either of us spoke about it. In our own way, each of us was beginning to ask, "Is this all there is?" Decorating the house, having friends in, martinis before dinner and other rituals—a project thrown in from time to time—was this it? Blanche was looking inward for spiritual answers and I was looking outward for career expansion. After all, my parenting days had ended and I felt free. Did I want to "marry" Blanche after having been married to the children's father, then to the children in terms of responsibilities, as well as having played the wife role to the doctor I left in Chicago? Did I want to start all over again? Whatever I sensed in her changes I was afraid to mention out loud. I was terribly jealous of Blanche and threatened by any small departure. She was so very attractive to others and I couldn't let go. Yet I yearned to cast my net wider and the opportunities seemed to be there. I began looking eastward,

eastward toward the Potomac, and before I knew it I was seriously involved with another woman—in fact, another woman who, like I was, had been in a committed relationship for years, but who had found new life in the liaison she and I had begun during my travels east.

1974-1976: The "Other Blanche"

I found my Potomac and much more.

San Francisco hadn't lost its charm for me but the routine life was beginning to get to me—drained of romance and bordering on celibacy. Son number two had taken off to attend a traditionally black college, departing from the "white life" he had lived both in San Francisco and Hyde Park. He complained that he needed to experience some black folk who were distinguished and learned and accomplished. There was this growing appetite in me also to take off—try myself as a black, educated and polished professional. Where might I do this? Where else? --In the nation's capitol. I had once met a woman from there at a professional meeting who was a high-ranking consultant for the Office of Health and Human Services. My next-door neighbor, a California psychologist and friend, was a huge admirer of hers so he eagerly made the connection for me, and within weeks I was airborne to my new landscape.

My first trip was certainly not final. After all, I couldn't—wouldn't—just jump up and leave my city by the Bay and the embers—not yet ashes—of my enviable relationship with the love of my life. No, the trip to D.C. began as an experiment. I was seeking opportunities, testing the waters with a big toe, but not with both feet. A lot was going on in the country in those days and opportunities abounded for such a person as I. Credentialed, acculturated, polished, and open, and the best part was that I was black and not one of the violent, screaming, vulgar blacks one saw on TV when watching the 6 o'clock news.

Ironically, the person in D.C. who took an interest in me was also named Blanche—a completely different kind of Blanche. My San

Francisco Blanche was an upper-class, Paris-born, Berkeley-bred nurse. My Washington Blanche had roots in the Amish community of Lancaster, PA and had relocated to Washington to accept a position with the federal government, but was also a nurse. Not in any way part of the Washington elite-- perceived at most as a bureaucrat, she hid her image behind a Sears Roebuck wardrobe and lived in a trailer camp. The shock sent me on a path of "working her over," changing her in exchange for the guidance and connections she was making for me in her geography.

That I did, starting with her obesity. She wasn't gross, as people look today, but she was indeed an unattractive heavyweight. Weight Watchers had not come into fashion in 1974, nor had Jenny Craig. The "other Blanche" and I had to do it on our own, and did she ever do it! For three months she ate nothing but tuna fish out of a can and grapefruits. She lost more than 100 pounds. Even her coworkers did not recognize her on certain days and had to do a double take when encountering her. The bottom line is that she fell in love with me during the process and I enjoyed the attention and the admiration that resulted from the changes in her. I also enjoyed the sex. She was a fantastic lover.

It was so spontaneous. On the first night of my time in D.C. she picked me up at my hotel and took me to her trailer park home. Somehow I sensed that she intended to be intimate and I did not resist. In fact, I wondered how she would pull it off. She was driving a tiny car—a Triumph III, TR-3 as it was called in that day. I was curious how such a big woman would be driving such a small car. En route she talked about how she had spent most of the night before cleaning and ordering the place, making it suitable for a guest. It was as though she expected me to accept her unspoken hospitality.

I had never been in a trailer camp before. I had never known anyone who lived in one. I had terrible images of trailer camp people—low-end whites who were failures in life, racists, unsophisticated, unexposed. It was a very big night; the first break in the fidelity of my mainline relationship with Blanche in California. The lovemaking was powerful. It erased my biases about fat people, trailer camp people, people from a religious background I had no way in Hell of understanding or appreciating. It erased almost everything in my life for the moment: the parenting, the joys of a refined and acculturated life in one of the most enviable and civilized cities in our country, and provided the feeling of freedom from a marriage regime. Yes, the lovemaking was so powerful that, for the moment, I forgot where I was and who I was. And all the days of our lives that were to follow presented an equally mysterious identity.

***

I was on a legitimate professional business trip in the nation's capitol, consulting for the Treasury Department; and I was on illegitimate "monkey business" in a rented apartment in Arlington, Virginia. The Christmas holidays were upon us and I had decided that if I offered my college student son and his cousin a trip to Washington for a special tourist type holiday, I could relieve my guilt about not making a family Christmas in California or returning to Chicago for the holiday.

It appeared to be working. The boys had agreed to come and I was dressing for the trip to National Airport.

She was puffing on her cigar in a corner of the room-very provocative. Her watchful eyes were full of lust. It was obvious that the simple and routine act of dressing myself was having a salacious effect on her.

"How can you look so sexy just putting on pantyhose?" She spoke through pursed lips.

"I didn't know I did."

I pointed my second toe into the other leg of the hosiery with a ballet-like movement. Flowing, I turned my back to her to hook on my bra. I didn't want to elicit more sexual tension between us. I had other things on my mind, like getting to National Airport to meet my son's plane, wondering how Christmas would be away from family, trying to entertain two teenage boys as I squired them around the mall, navigating the monuments and, of course, standing in that line of tourists awaiting entrance to the White House. No, this was no time to encourage intimacy!

So I briskly pulled my gray wool slacks over my hips and almost simultaneously yanked a matching turtleneck sweater over my head, completing the cover for both upper and lower body, and ending the moment of sexuality.

A Distraction: The Other Blanche

She was standing over her lover of ten years. She had driven wildly through the night from Washington, D.C. to Philly with a single purpose in mind. She must tell her about me. It was urgent. Her last sleepless night of tossing and turning would soon be history.

"Edith, something wonderful has happened to me and I pray you will understand and even appreciate it. No, I don't want any coffee. I just want to tell you so I can go back to breathing. I have been breathless for days.

"Edith, do you know the difference between loving and being in love? Of course you do. Why would I begin this with such a silly question? Bear with me; I'll get it out in a second. I love you and have for many years but now I'm in love. I have met someone who takes my breath away and gives it back to me at the same time—who literally has breathed new life into me, who has awakened feelings I thought were ling gone, maybe even created the feelings, whatever. They are new feelings. She makes me want to get up in the morning (yes, it is a she), makes me want to clean up the trailer, maybe even move out of that thing, sell it, give it away. She makes me want to change my entire lifestyle, throw away my dowdy Sears Roebuck dresses and yes, you guessed it, makes me want to lose weight.

"I can't believe it. I feel ten years younger and 50 pounds lighter and I haven't even lost a pound yet—but I'm going to."

Edith deserved to interrupt. She had been a good listener so far, and she very gingerly interrupted—

"Tell me, who is she? Where did she come from? Where did you find her? Sit down, tell me everything."

Edith began to sound like the good parent.

"First off, she's black AND gorgeous AND sexy AND a brilliant intellectual without being one of those erudite, boring snobs. Charm, she invented the word. She could charm the skin off a snake and sell ice to an Eskimo, as the sayings go… You know, Edith, we white folks do not know black people such as she exists. And especially not I, who grew up in that Amish culture in Lancaster. Edith, I see you frowning. Take off you social worker hat. If you're thinking that the novelty of her is what has gotten me crazy in love, you're wrong. She is not a toy or an adventure for me. She is the thing that is going to give me what I've never had: a love of self. Edith, did you know that I never really liked myself? And it's not just because I'm fat. It's because of everything I could be.

"There are complications. She lives in San Francisco with a partner of her own and has been doing some consulting work, which brought her to D.C. But, there is more to it. Her partner is an old relationship, solidly established what with an upscale condominium and a truly shared lifestyle. There's even a kid in the mix, but he's a teenager away in college at the time, which has helped free her to exploit her career. But, the dark side is that this long time lover of hers is beginning to explore herself, too, and her explorations are leading to that Born Again Christian thing.

"The situation is scary. You've heard about how crazy those Bay Area types can be. Shirley is cautious and committed to the California life, but there is no question that she is devouring my attention, excited about the potential in what might be open to her here in the nation's capitol, and fully responsive sexually. We have had great sex every minute we have been able to steal, and we can't keep our hands off each other. Nobody knows where any of this will take us, but right now we are both just floating in the discovery of each other and neither of us dares to think about the future."

Edith wept softly. The cigar smoker lit up and poured herself a jigger of brandy. She stays the night in Philly on Edith's couch.

Blanche: The Transition

She was acting differently. Usually, she would have warmly welcomed me with the almost desperate embrace of a needy, waiting lover, her body shifting from a quiver to a melt. Instead, the Blanche who met me at the San Francisco airport was a new Blanche, perfunctorily helping with the luggage after my trip east, hurrying to get home and not suggesting a pause in the airport lounge. I could sense that there would soon be a bottom-line statement.

I felt the anxiety building up in me. I was determined not to ask the questions frozen inside of me: "Is anything the matter, dear? You seem so hurried. Are you all right?" No, I was going to let whatever happened work its way out though I knew the oozing was destined to kill me.

This time, it was I who tried to decelerate the pace, a role usually assumed by Blanche.

> "Can't we have a drink while we wait for the luggage to come down? I deliberately did not have one on the plane. I was saving my thirst for you."

Blanche conceded, but it really felt like just a concession. The mood of celebration at my homecoming was not there.

* * *

I had begun to sense even before leaving on my trip east that Blanche was beginning to distance herself. Our martini before dinner ritual, which had been a joy for both of us, was eliminated from our day as exercising and dieting canceled that and our sit down meals with Peter. Blanche also had recently defected from the Catholic Church. We no longer attended Mass at the Cathedral and brunch at St. Francis. Little by little, the Blanche I had known was fading away. It was increasingly difficult to communicate with her. She spent more and more time in her room reading religious materials, and appeared depressed most of the time.

I think Blanche had begun to question the very life we were leading, but only hints of it came from her. She had not come out and said so. I believe she had begun to find it too materialistic. I had made a showplace of our condo, even hiring an interior decorator. We traveled, went skiing, threw parties, and dressed well. I was determined that we would not become like so many other same-sex couples—poor, out of fashion, rejecting family members and friends, isolating themselves.

I had been away from our San Francisco home for several months doing my consulting work on the east coast. My work with fundraising in the Bay Area had launched me to wider territories. Being educated at U of C enabled me to parlay my credentials, creativity, and writing skills into a successful career.

I had been across the country for consultations, seminars, and speeches, showcasing myself, leaving Blanche to find her own way. At first this was very exciting, even liberating, considering I had been tied down for years of wifely duties and parenting, but it often ended up feeling empty and impotent. All I wanted to do now was tell Blanche that what really mattered to me was carrying out our impossible dream. I intended to be home to stay.

* * *

We were finally seated in the airport lounge. I settled into a red leather chair and savored the moment. I loved Blanche—dark, swarthy complexioned Blanche, crowned by a mop of patent leather hair. Eyes more distinguished by their size than their color. Her big eyes were in fact a little too big for her face, slightly protruding, but engaging. The sweet sadness in them reflected the weight of deep thoughts, fiery passions, and the many other paradoxes within her that struggled for reconciliation. She was a Latin picture of seduction, a young adventuresome boy in a European woman's body.

She spoke first:

"A lot has happened to me lately. There's a church in Diamond Heights right up the hill from Safeway super mart. It's a little, unpretentious church. An Episcopalian pastor from Connecticut is the minister, but it's not really Episcopalian. It is a community church, and it encourages worship by all kinds of people. I've joined it and gotten involved. There was a tree planting ceremony while you were in Washington. I actually planted a tree! Can you imagine planting a tree?"

I felt old pangs of anxiety, the kinds I used to feel when Blanche would talk about a person too long, any person. My stomach folded and unfolded in a quiet turmoil. My mouth became dry and my eyes fixed as I searched for clues in every other word, every intonation, even in her breathing.

I listened and tried to show interest. My emotions belied all attempts. Blanche had been prone to many projects and movements, but nothing like this. Her projects had often put a distance between us. While she went through a project cycle, I was at an arm's length, no longer her center, out of her life for the duration. Was this to be another such project?

I felt anxious. Why did Blanche need this church? Did she want to get away from me and did not know how? Even in the luxury of the red leather chair, I squirmed.

"Tomorrow is Sunday, and I want you to see the church. Will you go with me to services?"

I agreed. There was no order for second drinks. I paid the check.

Together we went for the luggage, and then I waited on the curb for Blanche to bring the car out of the airport garage.

* * *

We entered the church on the high hill. The sun was unusually bright for this foggy city and everything seemed to sparkle but those happily miserable people who were the parishioners. They were a sorry lot: poor whites, crippled in either limb or in life, looking for each other, clinging--greeting and smiling and smelling of witch hazel. There were poor blacks on no particular track, satisfied to be part of the other group's pain, glad to be accepted, even though the common ground was shared addictions and rejections by others.

Suddenly, I felt sick, out of place among these losers. What did my lover need with this? I watched Blanche blending into a crowd of those as unlike her as they were unlike me. How lucky they all were to even know her! Little did they know…

Sitting obligingly in the pew of the church, I thought about our history together. I didn't care about the sermon or the people, and I had forgotten to look at the tree. From the side where I was seated, I would sneak a look at Blanche, who was actively participating in this stupid ritual. I watched her turn the pages of her missal, pointing to passages in the Good News Book and singing along with the congregation. I was careful not to let her catch me looking. Arrogant judgment possessed me.

I drifted into my best memories of Blanche. I had the dozens of love letters that sustained me during our times apart. The unending phone calls, and then that very special call saying she had purchased a brand new condominium for us on a very high hill in an area that reminded her of the Hyde Park neighborhood I would be leaving. The Thanksgiving weekend trip to San Francisco, which was planned to introduce me to the area to see if I really thought I could live there. Is there anyone who could not live in San Francisco in a beautiful new condo, and who is also in love? Of course there isn't. That weekend she had reserved a place on Fisherman's Wharf for us with a case of champagne, and she put a ring on my finger as well. She introduced me to her family at a traditional dinner and had given me the grand tour from Marin County's Sausalito to the rugged coast of Big Sur. I went back to Chicago mesmerized and determined to leave everything behind after that weekend.

Blanche was a great lover, a romantic and a naturalist. She taught me to count the stars in the skies over California, Nevada, and Oregon, where we frequently traveled. I was a sissy. I couldn't stand bugs or anything else of the outdoor life, but with her, everything was one big romance. She was fearless and honest about our love, but she offended no one. This born-again Christian freak she had become was a total stranger. It must be my fault.

Regardless, Blanche and I were finally over.

I returned to Chicago in 1979 to once again begin a new life. A life without women—reflective, responsible, with parenting, grandparenting and working among my priorities.

1999: Elaine, the Doctor/President

The telephone rang. It was 43 years after I had left Elaine. It was the same voice, but different somehow. There was more acid. I remembered that voice when it was throaty, low volume, breathy, sexy.

"Hello," from my kitchen.

"Hello," from Atlanta. "This is Elaine. How are you?"

"Well, hello. How are you, that is the question."

"I'm fine, just fine."

"Peter told me you had been quite ill."

"I wasn't sick. I had surgery."

There was a bit of acerbity inching into her voice. Through everything, there had been a kind of glue between Elaine and me that stuck us together over eons of time. She had been a part of all that went on in the lives of my sons—a positive thing. College graduations, law school graduations, weddings, honorary ceremonies, and career advancements took their place on the calendar right along side betrayals, accidents, and the tragic and fatal accident that killed her niece. So after more than four decades of being in and out of each other's lives, news of my surgery had brought this conversation to my kitchen phone. It was amazing that the same cold, defensive, unfriendly persona was evident which had characterized her stance forever, especially given that only a few years before we had been together to witness the grand ceremony of her inauguration to the Presidency of her Alma Mater.

I restrained myself, determined not to lead a verbal confrontation. What I wanted to say was, "What do you mean you weren't sick—how does one have major surgery without being sick?" That old lump began to rise like yeast in my middle. My restraints characterized our relationship way back then, not hers. After all, she was the doctor. Now she was the doctor and the President. Should her title be Mrs. President/Doctor or Mrs. Doctor/President?

"Well, I'm glad you're on the mend from whatever." I was congenial enough.

"Beth's family from Atlanta is here for Thanksgiving. And I saw Courtney last night. She loves Spelman."

(Shifting into neutral.)

"Who is Courtney?"

"Elaine's daughter, Beth's granddaughter."

"Oh, does she still live on campus?"

"No, she's awaiting a space. She's still at home."

"She's a transfer student then? That's why I don't know her. Well, tell her to stop by my office after she gets back and introduce herself to me."

The window of friendship was cracking open. I pried the window open a bit more, just enough to bring up the subject of my interest, Rachel, my granddaughter.

"While we're on the subject of Spelman, Rachel is applying for readmission for September 2000. She graduates from Parker in June. She had a huge struggle her first two years but her last report card was outstanding--in the beginning she wasn't prepared for the academic rigor of Parker...she came out of a Montessori elementary school where evaluation was not quantified."

I felt breathless. I was talking so fast, fearing not being able to finish, expecting her to interrupt, expecting impatience. I continued rushing to the end point but almost afraid to get there, the point where I would be asking something of her.

"She took the SATs but was not satisfied with her grade, so she took them again. I'm told she can take them as many times as she wants. When she gets the latest scores, she will make a formal application to Spelman.

"What we're thinking about is a campus visit. Peter says he'll meet her in Atlanta and do the tour with her and her mother plans to come, too. I know all campuses have tours all the time but I would hope that Rachel's time on campus might be a little special, given that you're the president. At least she would get to see you."

Then came the predictable interruption followed by a litany of policy statements regarding campus tours. How commonplace, how frequent, how arranged, and ending the discourse by directing me in a word to go through the proper channels. Not an intimate word, not even a personal comment. Strange for one who helped rear Rachel's father, was madly in love with me and suffered a clinical depression when I moved to San Francisco, separating her from Rachel's uncle Peter, who would come to be the closest she came to having a child of her own, and in whose life she remains dominant to this day. Strange she could not conjure up one single sentiment that connected Rachel to our stunning past!

Elaine, forever the doctor, forever in denial!

> "Well, whenever she takes the tour, I hope you'll be in town. Are you traveling much these days? Do you expect to be traveling in February? Rachel will have to come during her winter break from Parker, which is February 11-21."
>
> "I'm not traveling much now, but I don't know my February schedule."
>
> "That's okay, I can get that info later. There is still some time before February. Before I let you go, I want to tell you that I'm having hip replacement surgery next month. It is an old problem and for years I've been able to delay it with physical therapy and a mild regimen of medication, but lately the pain has become unbearable and I've made the decision to correct it."

My final restraint was not to say, "You must remember the hip, but you probably don't want to think about it. You must remember the morning you knocked me down in the basement of our house in a jealous rage while Peter slept upstairs. I fell hard on the right hip and went to the hospital the same day. Now you can rationalize that aging and normal degeneration has produced the problem, and in some way you are right. After all, I am 75 years old and somewhat arthritic and cartilage has worn away, but I have always related this hip problem to the fight in that basement." Harboring these thoughts had been the supreme restraint.

Part III:
Revelations

I have never understood what exactly happens to people when they claim to have "given themselves over to Christ," or "become a Christian," or "let God take over," or make any other pronouncements of revelation, such as "I've been saved." I only know what has happened to me as I look back on my odyssey. I must think about that "too wide" net. I must admit my burning passion, which was almost an obsession, to be different from everyone else, and I must confront my unrelenting determination to defy conventional wisdom at all costs only to be disappointed in the end by the very ones I fought for. Revelation has come to me in a roundabout way, and certainly not through the spiritual route. My transformation has been an in-your-face one, a "gotcha" one.

As my granddaughter grew under my nose into a stylistic lesbian caricature, without any lesbian interests or behavior, I could not just think that that look was the trend of the day; I thought, instead, if she was going to become "one of those." I worried as her dress became grubbier, and the extra pounds she put on so she could lump through the oversized clothes finished her off as the Good Housekeeping Stamp of Approval for the stereotypical 19th and 20th century dyke.

As my grandson showed real musical talent at the piano—loved to play, never had to be coaxed to practice, would even perch himself on a piano stool in a public place and watch the crowd gather—I began to wonder about him, too. "Is he going to become one of those?" I even contemplated genetic stuff, crazy stuff. Was a same-sex orientation in the genes? I thought about that paternalistic aunt of mine, Lucy, who could change a tire on the highway. I thought about any and every thing: back to Roy with the book under his sheets. I wondered, was it worth it? My own long life was so full of defiance and deviance.

I began to find fault with the orientation—the same-sex way of life. I never did like the culture: the politics, the demands, and the exhibitions. Living in the Bay Area and participating in groups I would often say, "Why, pray tell, do you guys have such a need to showcase your sexual preferences? Sexual orientation is a mere political phrase that wasn't even in the lexicon when I was a young thing. What more does it mean than 'who do you prefer as a bed partner?'" It means nothing and who do you think cares? Do others share with the world their most private moments? Hardly--and then they crossed the line. They not only wanted to eradicate abuse, obtain justice and equal access, they decided that they had the right to marry each other, "and by the virtue of the authority vested in the sacrament." With but a few word changes, their code sounds like the language in my University of Chicago diploma: "on the recommendation of the faculty and by the virtue of the authority vested in them the Trustees of the University have conferred…"

This is when my intrigue began to erode. Having denounced the traditional union between man and woman as a right, the gay community is demanding that the one institution which aims to make and keep us civilized, and to rein in our most basic urge to reproduce, namely marriage, is and should be up for grabs and any two can grab it under the guise of equal rights. That is when I felt my empathy melt away from gay and lesbian things. In spite of some of those things, I dearly loved and admired the aplomb of the women and the savvy of the men.

* * *

I go back and forth on my emotional roller coaster with the gay "thang," complaining, resenting, hating one day and enjoying and loving the next—much like a family. I feel grateful that I have other interests, other agendas, other "families." Now that I am unpartnered, totally detached, I can look back, and at times the recall is chilling.

The "gotcha" of my revelation came in a most unexpected way. An untimely death in my family took me away on a hiatus from my usual mental health career as a psychologist. I sought a distraction, something upbeat; I needed to be around some beauty and elegance and refinement. I needed to be around some beautiful people. So I talked myself into a job selling clothing for men at the high-end clothing store Neiman Marcus, on North Michigan Avenue. I knew I could do it even though I had no previous sales experience. I was familiar with the store. I had raised two boys, dressing men all my life.

I was perusing the merchandise on the second floor in the men's section, familiarizing myself with the swatches for the Oxxford suits when a dandyish sales associate of tenure literally hollered at me in a haughty tone, "Don't touch those!" I was shaken, embarrassed; this was just the beginning. This was one of the places where I had expected to find real camaraderie and ease. After all, these salesmen were all gay—which implies excessive refinement and manners—and I had my own lesbian "credentials" plus a lot of other attributes, the least of which was a PhD and broad travel experience.

Customers at NM found me to be knowledgeable, helpful, and engaging, especially mothers with their law school sons buying their first suit since bar mitzvah and wives helping their husbands who didn't want to be bothered with the gay salesmen. I was perfect for the job. But it was a paradox. Here I was: a black woman selling wear for men in competition with white gay men who identified with the store and its culture. I was a black woman who also identified with the store and its culture. I was sophisticated, educated, well-traveled, QE-2 and Concorde alum, and unpretentious. I had all the attributes that one could wish for in a store such as NM, all the attributes the customers could hope for in being served.

I was a black woman with lesbian credentials who wore them like a loose garment. Unstained, unmarked, but noticed by all and yet ignored by white male co-workers. "Black Woman, New Employee, Gets the Silent Treatment in Upscale Store!" Headlines, and in today's world! What goes there? I left after only a year and ran to my black gay male friends—especially to Paul.

Paul, I trusted my life with him. He mentored me through my graduate program at the University of Chicago, taught me to think analytically, and taught me to write, while I taught him to cook liver, which he had once detested. I was his wardrobe consultant, his travel companion, and when he decided to explore other neighborhoods—i.e. neighborhoods known to be user-friendly to gays and lesbians—he would tell me to put on my spaghetti-strap dress and my Chanel cloche and say, "Let's go out and create a little sexual tension."

* * *

Paul was my first neighbor in the building we had to vacate because the U of C was establishing the Lutheran Seminary on that site. The gossip mill told me he was a PhD student on a Kellogg Foundation fellowship, transplanted from a traditionally black, legendary college: Tuskegee Institute in Alabama. The gossip mill also told that Paul was a gay man—a term that had not truly worked its way into the lexicon in the 1950s. I just knew he was different from other Negro men.

For example, his lifestyle impressed me. He went swimming every day, he enjoyed foreign travel, he had many white friends and he was superbly intelligent. It was impossible to be with him for even a short time without learning something. He had style and he was handsome. His aquiline nose and high forehead set above gray-green eyes disguised his Negroid ethnicity. He could have been a member of any number of racial groups. I was glad to hear that he may be gay. I could then seek his companionship without being concerned about the gender play between the sexes; all those games need not be played. Further, my own living arrangements with a woman ten years my junior, and a doctor at that, would not be so curious to him as we developed a friendship.

Of course I was delighted to find that he was a scholar and that we had the U of C in common—he on the PhD level, I on the Masters level. We became very good friends and traveled together from time to time: short trips to places in Illinois noted for their historic interest and one very big trip to Mexico where my partner and I joined him for a beachside and city side holiday, in Acapulco and Mexico City. It was wonderful traveling to a foreign country with one who had been there before and knew the language.

While learning by association came naturally with Paul, here were some very specific things we taught each other. He thought I, too, had style and panache and I soon became his fashion and entertainment "consultant." It was so engaging and so much fun there were times I could ignore Elaine's philandering. He was good for my sons. There were no thoughts of improprieties. Sexual abuse? The threat of it? The fear of it? No way. That just wasn't in the cards in my friendship with Paul. In looking back I often wonder, was that a "white thang?"—looking back to my own childhood, occasionally I would spend the night away from home at my aunt and uncle's house and it was quite commonplace that I might sleep in their bed. Neither of them ever touched me! Once I felt something hard, like a baseball bat, pressing against my leg. When I became old enough to understand that it was probably my uncle's penis, it was just something I understood and it did not require any discussion.

Once my alliance with Paul caused a major split in my relationship with Elaine. It was the night King was assassinated and outraged black folk began burning up the west side of Chicago. Paul and I were on one side of the issue and Elaine was on the other. She was most empathetic to their behavior. Paul and I thought it stupid and refused to wear the symbolic black band on our arms the next day to school. This was just one of the many splits between Elaine and me.

* * *

Oh, how I miss Paul. Were he still alive, I bet he would help me resolve this conflict about the NM store. He would sit me down at the kitchen table and say:

> "Now, now. We're going to have to put this into a conceptual framework, just like at U. of C. It needn't be so worrisome. Just listen. You've had great personal experiences and you have been intrigued with the deviance and the otherworldliness of people like me. You have associated their personas and their lifestyles with intelligence, creativity, art, and pizzazz. You also enjoy their vigorous spirit, energy and excitement. All in all, these are the characteristics not typical of our race. You have long rejected

your blackness—as did your mother and your aunts (remember, I knew your mother, and loved her, I can still taste those pies she baked for Walter and me.).

"Then you have a bad experience. You're rejected, probably for the first time in your life. A bunch of racist sissies who behave like their rich customers—talking Opera, and the Lyric season exotic travel and the like to impress them—and all of a sudden the likes of you appear on the scene. You were competing with them on the sales floor, out-selling them, seeing through them and their shenanigans. Next, their inborn, inbred racism surfaces and takes over. They cannot see you as an interesting deviant, an enigma, an interesting puzzle—the way you would have liked to be seen. No, they see you as a threat and they are not quite sure why. So they leave you alone, stay clear, hoping you will go away.

"In your naïveté you can't see this so you are ready to denounce the entire species, including me. But, you love me, so you can't put that in the mix. Yes, this whole game was more fun and classier before the rules of justice and equality entered, before it became mainstream and Main Street. There was intrigue to plunge into an unknown. There was calculated risk in flirting in a public place with an innocent bystander. You got a response, or you did not, and the goal was not the bedroom. It was just making the connection. If a bedroom was in the offering, it came much later and after elaborate preparations.

"Shirley, you are not a lesbian. You are an explorer. An adventurer, that's what you are! An aspirant to the high culture--and you thought the way to get there was through deviant sex. You are anti-black. That's all."

* * *

And now the end is near and my thoughts turn to the signature song of my favorite performer—who else but ole "Blue Eyes?" Yes, he said it all in "My Way." It seems years and miles away from that consultation room in Northwestern Memorial Hospital where I listened with my family to the medics tell me that the surgery was imminent and that I should prepare for the worst and hope for the best. My idea was to write down all that I could remember about my life. I lived through the surgery. I lived through the "Writing Down the Bones"—to quite the wonderful how-to book by Natalie Goldberg. So now I must live through the memories and the consequences.

Appendix:
New Revelations

It is so commonplace it's almost a cliché. This thing of looking back at the road not taken or a person or persons who dominated your life. It usually comes at the end of life when we seem to revel in retrospective mode. And it comes in many forms; sometimes the focus is on a person and we are astounded to remember how we cried for that person, feared that person, and went to extreme ends to please that person. Other times we are amused and laugh at ourselves when we remember how one affected us as such. If we have outlived someone who was once central to our well being, that's a surprise. I have outlived all but two of those people.

This retrospective thinking, this looking back, is a process, and when you start it you rarely know where it's going to take you or when it will end. With me it began with a last ditch attempt to fashion a very unrealistic love affair with Kathleen: like an old man buying a 2-seater sports car when his joints are curled and he lacks the agility to straddle the console mounted between the bucket seats. But he lets the top down and sails on up Rush Street and the Magnificent Mile or Rodeo Drive or Ocean Avenue.

Happily, Kathleen in her wisdom helped me begin the process by rejecting my advances. She hardly spoke a word, just didn't respond. Failed to answer my letters (and I wrote voluminously); but through it all she kept up the platonic side of the relationship. She kept it alive while she waited for me to regain consciousness—to surface from my emotional coma. She became a truly staunch friend in every single way. She drove me to medical appointments, Bridge games, played Bridge as my Partner. She introduced me to AA meetings (when I thought I might have had a drinking problem as a result of a single episode in which I experienced a "blackout"—but later decided that I didn't need those Meetings), participated in events of my family. For example, she accompanied me to my son's home for a Birthday Dinner, and included me in several events with her family. What more could I wish for?

The process moved the gears up a notch. I began to feel "normal" in her presence. No longer anxious. Not constricted. I was beginning to free myself. I thought if I could find something "wrong" with her—something unappealing, distracting, like a double chin or a lumbering, heavy walk—it would be easier for me. But no negatives could trump that gloriously coifed white hair that fell in a wave over her right eye and crowned her elegant head in a Spencer Tracy-type style, or the jaunty air of her appearance when she planted a French beret on top, angled to one side. I gave up the fruitless task of looking for flaws.

A telephone call from my very first live-in lover—and now retired Physician, retired Asst. Surgeon General, and more recently, retired College President—shook me up a bit. Our relationship, even after we tore our lives apart, had continued to be testy so I was surprised by a call from her. She was asking me a favor, after 50 years. She was selling her Jamaican property (a second home), and needed me to track down the Chicago lawyer who had sold it to her years ago. It was a tax issue. I agreed to look in all the right places and within days I was able to report his demise some five years ago. That call moved my retro processing even a further notch up. I remembered the song and began to chant it: "If I met you today…would I be led astray"—and the chant took me back to all the others: the others before Kathleen, long before Kathleen. The other women. The other places. The other roads taken and not taken. The other moves. The living and the dead. Lil, the outrageous scandalized woman who caused my own mother to reject me. The English Teacher who gave me the first kiss after Graduation from High School—the "kiss of death" which stayed on my lips for years. Bernice, the

University of Chicago Visiting Professor from Wisconsin who drove to Chicago to take me back to her Wisconsin apartment—a three plus hour trip because she was "hot for me" on a particular night. Sylvia, the intellectual whose life I changed through my love. The Other Woman. Of course, Elaine, whose love for me was a closeted travesty. And finally Blanche, my idol, who gave me the opportunity to prove to the world that Love is Not Gender Specific—and the opportunity to do that in the most beautiful and exciting place in the United States—San Francisco!

Then Kathleen—my end of life love who taught me to love unconditionally; without carnal appetite. Kathleen, who gave me "The Other Woman."

And so I also enclose several of my letters to Kathleen, to give the world a small piece of this chapter of my life.

* * *

May 5, 2005

Dear Kathleen,

Before you read this, I would like you to know a bit about the "storyline" and the Revelation. It is truly a story of my life that is intended to portray the many facets of it—thus rendering me "normal."

I reject the "lesbian" label and all things lesbian. I reject the categorization and spend time and effort disputing it—then, after my friend Paul lectures to me and I have had the unhappy experience in the Neiman Marcus store, I finally accept his theory that racism overrides all gender issues.

Then, out of the blue, I am struck by a bombshell: you, and at "old-age" I begin a doomed wooing through a series of letters to you until, finally, I realize that I can't have you as a lover but only as a friend. The greater realization is that I may be a lesbian after all.

* * *

November 20, 2004

Dear Ms Johnston,

I would wager that in your illustrious career you have never received a letter such as I am crafting here. It is a most unusual piece of correspondence and for me — taken in context — it just might be thought of as a "high risk" letter, dependent upon how it is interpreted. Some idiots in our society might dare to call it 'harassment"-- idiots who don't even know how to pronounce the word! Here goes--:

I was a participant in the Retirement Workshop on November 18 in which you were the third and last speaker and spoke on "Death & Taxes". I am also the member of the group whom you may have noticed left early. (I did not leave early to avoid the test: I had another appointment —smile). To further identify me, I was the one in the group who interspersed the quotation--"One man and one woman"--the comment that got a rise out of the group, including yourself.

I should have left before you came on as a speaker because early on I was made to realize that Retirement was not relevant to my particular situation and Retirement was what the entire agenda was about. Why? Because I cannot "retire" until I have worked in the system a minimum of eight years; and unhappily I interpreted the "Rule of 85" to mean that I could add the four years I have been with the State to my age (older than Christ), 81, and come up with the number needed for retirement. Well, I was wrong and I should have walked out of the door within the first hour.

Had I done that, I would have missed the wonderful presenters of information that did not serve me but was nevertheless interesting — information I plan to pass on to my adult children. More to the point, had I left when I should have I would have missed you and that would have been a real loss. I want to spend the remainder of this letter describing myself and what has dominated my thoughts since I experienced you in the hopes that you just might be interested in getting to know me better and accepting a dinner invitation from me.

First off, I am inappropriately assigned to The Office of the Secretary of State in the CIL (Chicago Information Line) department. This happened because after 40 years of Psychology private practice — consultancies, teaching, and Consultant roles, I was plagued with life threatening heart surgery and gave up my formal professional career. My surgery was truly "life-threatening." I had an aneurysm in the aorta and, in a word--I was bleeding to death. The surgery lasted 13 hours and no one expected me to survive it. Since I did, and since my family knew Jesse White, I was given a job answering the telephone in a building--the former Chas A. Stevens store for Women--the predecessor to today's Neiman Marcus--and, the store that gave me my very first credit card, located at 17 North State Street. So, there is where I am today.

In that setting I have experienced "culture shock" to the "nth degree." You could not even imagine how it hurts my ears to hear the language and observe the dress and hairstyles and otherwise dissonant things I experience everyday. Therefore, because I have the Medical History needed to qualify for a Leave of Absence I shall be taking that beginning January, 2005. Now, on to my next subject and the one that may get your interest In addition to having been a Psychologist-- a REAL Psychologist, not a Community College student who took Psychology #101-- I am a born writer. If the world had been different when I was a growing child and adolescent, I would have become either a Hemingway or a Mike Royko-- depending upon whether or not I was a storyteller or a journalist. But the world was not ready for a little black girl from the south side of Chicago who wanted to write. Write about what? Those who would have interviewed me might have said. I would have been like Obama is today--"a skinny black guy with a funny name from the south side of Chicago." Except today is ready for an Obama. The 1930s and 1940s were not ready for a Shirley Simeon-- and the world was certainly not ready for the subject matter I was interested in.

Today I have a completed manuscript, which I am hoping to get published. I also have 32 plus Commentaries and Op-Ed articles-- some of which have been published in Chicago papers and magazines, magazines including *Playboy*. So, when I leave my SOS job the first of the new year I intend to spend my time marketing myself. Making contacts with people like yourself who might take an interest in me Exploiting (tastefully, the opportunities that may lead to something!) However, this letter which may represent a "making-of-contacts" is more than that. It will be difficult for me to explain what I must but I shall try.

When I first glimpsed you walking along the wail on the side of the room #505, you struck me like a bolt of lightening—"who is she?" What a sexy, glamorous, elegant lady--I now know why the song was written--"Love is wasted on the young." At that point in the Workshop I had to stay. And, I stayed until I had to leave. What is so significant to a Psychologist (me) is why, pray tell, why have I for the past three days never gotten you off my mind? What has that to say about you and me? Let me continue: Did you look like my therapist of old? Yes, a little. Might the two of you be related? She too had gorgeous white hair, a similar body-type and "flashing" eyes. She was and is, Jewish. I am not certain that you may be—but that really doesn't matter. What matters is why I haven't been able to get you off my mind since that Workshop.

Why did I miss writing down your State telephone number and never needing to write down your name and then going to the Chicago telephone book expecting — not only to find you in it but to find you in the neighborhood where you are — talk about "profiling"!! I could look at you-- you reeked class and guess that you did not live in the "burbs" and if in the City, it would have been exactly where you do live. Why did all these things come together in one fell swoop? I am sure you now know why I spoke of this kind of a letter as a "high risk" communication. You could easily decide that, "here is a person who became smitten with me with no provocation from me and may be dangerous."

Why am I not worried that you would do that? First off, I am leaving State employment as of the end of this year and my job or my career cannot be affected by such a communication. Second, and I haven't mentioned this before--you and I have something in common: The University of Chicago. Also, I have a son who is a lawyer and a brother who was so effective as a Civil Rights Lawyer in Texas that a huge edifice — a Library has been erected in his name --- and my entire family ceremoniously traveled to Texas some years ago for the dedication. Just for the records, you might want to check this out his name was Elmo Willard from Beaumont Texas. His son, David Willard is now a PhD student at Harvard University. I tell you these things so that you may be comfortable in being in touch with me and extending our time. Also so that I may tie up my writing with the elements of our meeting.

I have written a book about the commonality and the normalcy of same-sex relationships. Using my own life script as an example. I was married, had two sons (who are very normal men living very normal lives). Moreover, I had major relationships with women who were not by definition "lesbian." Normal women, so-to-speak. The point of my book is to illustrate that LOVE IS NOT GENDER SPECIFIC.

If you are not "blown away" by this very revealing writing, and would like to meet me in a social situation, it could be fun to explore why, oh why have I become so smitten with you not even knowing you. I enclose a resume so that you can see that I am a credible person-- not because I am looking for a job.

Happy Holidays and I will be very disappointed if I don't hear from you.

Very sincerely,

Shirley R. Simeon, PhD

* * *

Dear Kathleen,

I have determined from our casual conversations that we really do have a lot in common. It is uncanny how many things we have done in a similar way — like "crossing the Atlantic" alone as we both did. I on the QE-2 -- I don't remember you telling me your route. We seem to both enjoy many of the same kinds of recreational activities — theatre, Museum memberships, Symphony memberships, travel (especial spontaneous travel) --you told me that you, like myself always pack at the last minute! I am convinced that there is some mysterious reason that we should have crossed each other's paths.

For the years that I have left, I would like to explore those reasons. Of course, I am probably much too old to attract you as a sexual entity; but I am glad that you allowed me to express the attraction. At this point in my life I would be satisfied at having you as a special friend with whom I can do things I enjoy — and, more than that, to use my attraction for you as an antidote against other distractions that may get in the way of really what I want to do and can do well — write. It may sound "silly" but it thrills me to enter a room and see you sitting as you were today, waiting for me, reading a book.

After you read my Manuscript draft which will be in your hands on May 1 — no later, I hope you will find it both interesting and somewhat riveting. After your trip to Paris, I hope we can sit down together in either your place or mine and talk about what the story means and how I can benefit from its publication. Moments like I anticipate once we settle in to accepting ours as a special relationship, I will be more relaxed and less unrealistic about any sexual aspects of what we now have. What would I like to happen? I would like for us to continue to work on a partnership for Bridge.

I would like for you to show some indication that you want to be with me and invite me to do some of the things you do either alone, or with another. I would like for you to think of me as having a special place in your life and to feel comfortable about sharing me with your friends. I have no problem (and I believe I have said this before) with you talking to others in your life who care about you and letting my image, my letters, my proposals be known to others in your life whom you trust not to make a scandal out of my letters.

This is a pure guess: I have no data on what I am about to suggest: I would wager that in this world of "ordinary people" there are a good many who would like to have someone such as I "in love" with them. I hope my being "in love" with you gives you a smile. More later.

Shirley

* * *

April 26, 2005

Kathleen,

During weekends before I met you, often I would be alone in my little apartment. Unlike you, I do not tend to be a "hermit-personality." Yet I have not fully adjusted to the life I have now as a semi-retired person — nor have I adapted to the life of a grandparent. In an earlier life, I was an "Auntie Mame" type grandparent. Therefore I have resumed my writing life and because it has been autobiographical it has turned the spotlight on reflection of an earlier life. Happily you entered my life and became (through no fault of your own -- smile — an emotional anchor. I needed you — for my life and for my book. Even my editor agrees. While you have yet to read the book the essence of it describes a person — the protagonist —who has spent her life protesting arid fighting against the issues of "lesbianism." "There is no such thing!" she cries. She proves her position by having affairs with "normal" women who have no stigma of lesbianism — and with living a fairly normal life as a conventionally married person and a parent.

Then at the end of her life she discovers that after all she just may be a "lesbian" because she falls in love with the likes of a Kathleen. And this is no small thing.

Now, back to the present: I am much too old as I have told you before — regardless of how I look and act — for you to develop any sexual interest in me; though you and I both know that sexual appetites and sexual fulfillment have no chronological age. Yet I found in you a "soul mate" — one who can finish my sentences, who seems to have shared many of my experiences and with whom we speak the same language despite our racial differences. And, needless to say, I eroticized those findings. I thought they would lead to a common bed, if you will. They led to a table: a Bridge table and it appears that that is enough. They also led me to the conclusion of my book — which my editor loves!

So, I can tonight announce that I have given up on the notion of pursuing you as a lover. I will continue to pursue you as an intimate friend who will forgive me for my lust and, should it ever present itself, would not be afraid to tell me if you may ever have experienced any feelings of "lust" for me. Or for anyone else in your vast experiences in the life you have led.

This letter to you supercedes all previous ones and is the most candid and honest written communications I have ever fashioned.

Love ya,

Shirley

About the Author

My entire career has been driven and advanced by my innate talent for writing. At age 15 my high school English teacher identified this and wrote to my Mother in 1938 that she should nurture and encourage it but I chose career paths that promised economic security and even a bit of prestige for a black child born in racist America in the 1920s and attending high school in the 1930s. So after forty plus years as a professional teacher, social worker, and finally Psychologist, writing for others - my bosses, my professors, et al, I have finally settled into writing for myself and writing about myself, and above all writing about a subject dear to my heart.

All academic pursuits led to this subject -- Gender, and its ramifications. Loyola University at Chicago gave me a Jesuits' philosophical foundation earning a PhB degree there - which was an enigma kind of credential - and worth little on the job market place. But having been one of the few black graduates in the class of 1946, gave me some distinction. White girls in great numbers were not finishing college in that year. Twelve years, 2 marriages, 2 children and a "creative" divorce (a term yet to be launched in the vernacular) freed me to again return to my passion for writing. Only this time I was going to "put my money where my mouth was" and live out the "gender thing". I had added a supplement - labeling. Gender with a twist; Gender with an attitude. Down with labels! "Don't you dare try to peg me".

I honed my writing skills, through work as one of Richard J.'s lieutenants and "cabinet members" in the illustrious Chicago Poverty Program - a model for the nation in 1965, and added a Master's Degree from The University of Chicago then I took off to San Francisco, where I lived my beliefs with a same-sex partner and my teen-age son. Leaving a conservative, supportive, Catholic family behind, and a family-system I had endured and loved for a lifetime, I said my Chicago goodbyes in a most elegant venue - the Seven Continents Restaurant at O'Hare airport. Armed with prestigious degrees, a flair for writing, and a "black-is-beautiful" mantra of the 1960s I felt confident that I could change the world about Gender. At age 83 I am still trying.

Printed in the United States
58865LVS00003B/82-99